PHENOMENOLOGY

Other interview books from Automatic Press ♦ⱽᵢP

Formal Philosophy
edited by Vincent F. Hendricks & John Symons November 2005

Masses of Formal Philosophy
edited by Vincent F. Hendricks & John Symons October 2006

Philosophy of Technology: 5 Questions
edited by Jan-Kyrre Berg Olsen & Evan Selinger February 2007

Game Theory: 5 Questions
edited by Vincent F. Hendricks & Pelle Guldborg Hansen April 2007

Philosophy of Mathematics: 5 Questions
edited by Vincent F. Hendricks & Hannes Leitgeb January 2008

Epistemology: 5 Questions
edited by Vincent F. Hendricks & Duncan Pritchard September 2008

Philosophy of Medicine: 5 Questions
edited by J. K. B. O. Friis, P. Rossel & M. S. Norup September 2011

Intellectual History: 5 Questions
edited by Morten Haugaard Jeppesen, Frederik Stjernfelt & Mikkel Thorup May 2013

The History of Logic in China: 5 Questions
edited by Fenrong Liu & Jeremy Seligman September 2015

Science and Religion: 5 Questions
edited by Gregg D. Caruso March 2014

Peirce: 5 Questions
edited by Francesco Bellucci, Ahti-Veikko Pietarinen & Frederik Stjernfelt July 2014

Social Epistemology: 5 Questions
edited by Duncan Pritchard and Vincent F. Hendricks, January 2015

Images: 5 Questions
edited by Aud Sissel Hoel, Peer Bundgaard and Frederik Stjernfelt, Febuary 2016

See all published and forthcoming books in the 5 Questions series at
www.vince-inc.com

PHENOMENOLOGY: FIVE QUESTIONS

EDITED BY

FELIPE LEÓN

JOONA TAIPALE

Automatic Press ♦ VP

Automatic Press ♦ V̲I P

Information on this title: www. vince-inc. com

© Automatic Press / VIP 2018

This publication is in copyright. Subject to statuary exception and to the provisions of relevant collective licensing agreements, no reproduction of any part may take place without the written permission of the publisher.

First published 2018

Printed in the United States of America
and the United Kingdom

ISBN-10 / 87-92130-58-5
ISBN-13 / 978-87-92130-58-7

The publisher has no responsibilities for the persistence or accuracy of URLs for external or third party Internet Web sites referred to in this publication and does not guarantee that any content on such Web sites is, or will remain, accurate or appropriate.

Cover design by Vincent F. Hendricks

Contents

Preface	v
Acknowledgements	vii
1. Renaud Barbaras	1
2. Rudolf Bernet	11
3. John B. Brough	21
4. David Carr	33
5. Steven Crowell	39
6. Françoise Dastur	49
7. Nicolas de Warren	57
8. John Drummond	67
9. Günter Figal	77
10. Shaun Gallagher	87
11. Miguel García-Baró	91
12. Sara Heinämaa	101
13. Nam-In Lee	109
14. Dermot Moran	121
15. Tetsuya Sakakibara	135
16. Anthony J. Steinbock	141
17. Bernhard Waldenfels	155
18. Dan Zahavi	167
About the Editors	175

Preface

♦

In the opening lines of his *Phenomenology of Perception* (1945) Merleau-Ponty ponders the fact that still, after half a century from Husserl's first writings, there exists as-yet no consensus on what phenomenology amounts to. In many ways, these words are still topical: the discussion on the nature of phenomenology still rages both inside and outside the phenomenological tradition. In the analytic philosophical tradition, phenomenology has been linked with idealism and introspectivism. In post-structuralist thought, phenomenology has often been viewed as something like Wittgenstein's ladder: a necessary stepping stone that one should nonetheless eventually dispense oneself with. Within phenomenology, to mention one of the most salient foci of disagreement, the debate on the relationship between the Husserlian and Heideggerian versions of phenomenology has been under intense discussion during the past century – and the situation is not made any easier by the fact that even Husserl and Heidegger themselves developed their views on what phenomenology amounts to in the course of their careers.

It is thus only fitting, we think, that the issue about the nature of phenomenology is also approached in a somewhat non-standard way. Continuing the 'Five Questions' series in philosophy, the present volume comprises central insights about that issue from some of the most prominent scholars in contemporary phenomenology. The contributions to the volume, however, are not primarily argumentative attempts to clarify what phenomenology objectively is, but rather writings on what phenomenology has meant for these individual scholars. The format of the contributions, conceived as responses to a five-question questionnaire, has allowed each author to address in a concise and flexible way a broad range of topics, from personal reflections on how each of them was drawn into phenomenology, to considerations about the latter's significance in the contemporary intellectual landscape. The result is a volume containing insightful and thought-provoking reflections about the past, present, and future of phenomenology from outstanding scholars in the field.

While many other scholars could obviously have been included in the volume, we believe that the eighteen contributions that we have gathered are representative of the diversity of routes that have led people to adopt a phenomenological grip on many foundational philosophical questions. All in all, the contributions draw together a rather wide picture of phenomenology, even if not a comprehensive and exhaustive one, and they testify for the richness of the phenomenological tradition.

The individual contributions are not all alike. In the spirit of the format adopted in the Five Questions series, we have given the contributors the option to reply to the five questions one by one, or in the form of a differently structured contribution.

The five questions we posed were the following:

1. Why were you initially drawn to phenomenology?
2. What are your main contributions to the field of phenomenology?
3. What is the proper role of phenomenology in relation to other disciplines?
4. What have been the most significant advances in phenomenology?
5. What are the most important open problems in phenomenology and what are the prospects for progress?

Copenhagen & Jyväskylä, October 2018
Felipe León & Joona Taipale
Editors

Acknowledgements

We are grateful to the contributors for accepting with kindness and generosity our invitation, and to the VIP/Automatic Press for making the appearance of this volume possible. We would also like to thank the following persons and institutions: Dan Zahavi, Vincent F. Hendricks, Henrik A. Boensvang, the Center for Subjectivity Research, the University of Copenhagen, and the University of Jyväskylä. Joona Taipale's funding for the editorial work was provided by the Kone Foundation and the University of Jyväskylä, and Felipe León was funded by the University of Copenhagen.

Copenhagen & Jyväskylä, October 2018
Felipe León & Joona Taipale
Editors

1

Renaud Barbaras

Professor, Chair of Contemporary Philosophy
Paris 1 Panthéon-Sorbonne (France)
Translated from French by Felipe León

---

1. Why were you initially drawn to phenomenology?
My discovery of phenomenology coincided more or less with that of philosophy. When I was seventeen, in graduating class, I had read Merleau-Ponty and then Heidegger, whom I didn't understand much. It is worth underlying that at that time, dominated by the philosophies of suspicion (Nietzsche, Marx, Freud), being interested in phenomenology, and, moreover in Merleau-Ponty – a period of stagnation in the reception of his work had begun – was not at all to be taken for granted. During my studies of philosophy, I certainly turned to other authors, and began working on the metaphysics of Leibniz. What interested me was basically the side of his metaphysics that didn't draw only on logic: the topics of creation, the monade, compossibility, in brief, the issue of contingency. Now it appears to me clearly, as Merleau-Ponty saw it very early, that one finds there a set of ideas that converge with the phenomenological perspective. After this detour through classical metaphysics, I very rapidly had the feeling that those questions that mattered to me the most, and that I had believed could be addressed within that framework, could only be dealt with within phenomenology. I read Husserl's *Ideas*, and I was fascinated by the thematic of the reduction, as well as by the eidetics of the perceived. I then discovered Merleau-Ponty's *The visible and the invisible*, the reading of which was a major event for me. The drafted part and, even more, the working notes – which more than thirty years later haven't lost for me their extraordinary brilliance – seemed to me to open up a path of incredible fertility. I quickly decided to devote my thesis to Merleau-Ponty, more specifically to the ontology sketched in that posthumous work[1]. In a certain way, everything I have written since then has its source in that initial work of mine, and proceeds from the attempt of going as far as

---

[1] Renaud Barbaras, *De l'être du phénomène Sur l'ontologie de Merleau-Ponty*, Grenoble, J. Millon, 1991, 2001.

possible along the way opened up by Merleau-Ponty. Such an attempt also implied highlighting the difficulties in his project, and thus also a certain distancing from it.

2. What are your main contributions to the field of phenomenology?

I leave aside my contributions to the history of phenomenology, even if, of course, they were indispensable for working out my own perspective. My contributions can be summarized in four works: two of them deal with Merleau-Ponty[2], and two with Jan Patočka[3], the reading of whom was certainly the second big event in my pathway in phenomenology, and the decisive step in the constitution of my own position.

(1) I tried to take charge as radically as possible of the double demand that the determination of the meaning of being of the subject of the correlation, i.e. ultimately, of intentionality, hinges upon. On the one hand, the subject radically differs from the world as long as he commands the appearance of the latter. On the other hand, however, he radically belongs to the world, he exists as a being in the world. This double demand is brought together in the Merleau-Pontyan notion of flesh: the latter is indistinctively my flesh, without which no world would appear, and flesh of the world. I showed, however, that this concept remained equivocal, that it didn't allow to truly think the solidarity between the belonging and the difference, in so far as the flesh remains divided by the partition between the sensing and the world, where the duality prevails over the unity. The question is thus the following: how can the subject, *from the same point of view*, belong to the world and differ from it? Or also: in what sense can the difference of the subject involve his belonging, and his belonging involve his difference? I have shown, relying on a critique of intuitionism and of that which persists of substantalism, not only in Husserl but also in the majority of his successors, that the only way to satisfy this demand is to think the subject as movement, and thus to understand phenomenology as a *dynamic* phenomenology. Indeed, as movement, the subject radically differs from other beings: the movement is a concrete negation of substantiality, the only way not to be oneself, and as a consequence, it sets a distance from the world as a totality of beings. Nonetheless, on the other hand, there is no movement without a ground for its deployment. As an active and concrete negation, the movement requires the positing of a space that sus-

---

[2] The referenced work is *Le tournant de l'expérience - Recherches sur la philosophie de Merleau-Ponty*, Paris, Vrin, 1998, 2009.

[3] *Le mouvement de l'existence. Etudes sur la phénoménologie de Jan Patočka*, Ed. de la Transparence, 2007. *L'ouverture du monde. Lecture de Jan Patočka*, Ed. de la Transparence, 2011.

tains it. To put it differently, there is movement only within a world: its difference *vis-à-vis* the beings presupposes its belonging to the world of which these beings are the manifestation. Thus, from the same point of view, that of movement, the subject differs radically from the world and profoundly belongs to it. From the point of view of movement, there is no alternative between being *in front* of the world, as a condition of appearance of the latter, and finding itself *in* it.

Of course, if the sense of being of the subject has to be characterized as movement, the latter is movement of a subject, or rather it merges with the subjective existence, i.e. with the activity of phenomenalization. This is therefore a very peculiar movement, that unites an active belonging to the world and an experiencing of the world. This movement is nothing but the movement of *life*, and that is the reason why the dynamic phenomenology that I have tried to elaborate can be characterized as a *phenomenology of life*. It suffices to hear life in its original sense, more profound than the partition between an intransitive life (being alive, *leben*) and a transitive life (to live something, to make the experience of something, *erleben*). This amounts to saying that the subject can live the world, i.e. make the experience of the world, only under the condition of existing as a living being within the world, and that, inversely, there is no living being, no matter how simple, that is not already a subject, susceptible of relating itself to the world. The first consequence of this discovery is, evidently, the impossibility of attributing to the human being alone the power of making the world appear. The human being is a subject because it is a living being, and the question that has to be posed then is what distinguishes the human from other living beings, as long as all of them relate to the world. Ultimately, I was led to call *desire* this movement that is at the heart of life, so that the phenomenology of life is a phenomenology of desire. In fact, on the one hand, desire is characterized by the fact that it only makes its object (the desired) appear in advancing toward it. Desire only unveils its object while approaching it. It is, ultimately, a phenomenalizing movement or a phenomenalization that takes the shape of a movement. On the other hand, desire is distinguished by the fact that that which satisfies it exacerbates it, instead of filling it in, in such a way that, to put it that way, it nourishes from itself and can only access any appeasement in death. Now, this is absolutely in conformity with the status of that which is desired by the desire, i.e. phenomenalized in and by its movement, namely the world itself. Indeed, from a perspective that owes to Eugen Fink as much as to Merleau-Ponty, it has to be underlined that the world is that which presents itself in every being always as an excess, as a depth that is at the same time unassignable and irreducible. The world is that which every being manifests, the foundation from which it comes, or the stuff from which it is made, but that never presents itself. It differs from beings without being anything else but them (if it were it would still be a being): it is an internal excess within the being, a pure transcendence that is not the transcendence of a transcendent. Now, to a world that always exceeds presence can only be suitable a subject that is its own excess, that is as if overflown by itself. The world is that which is targeted by the desire, that which is desired by every desire. By its own fault, it cannot give itself but in the form of that or that finite being, and that is why the movement through which the world appears is without end and rest. Therefore, that which desire achieves is never that which it desires. Satisfaction always remains dissatisfaction. Thereby, within the framework of the dynamic phenomenology (or phenomenology of life, or of desire) that I have tried to elaborate, the static correlation between consciousness and world leaves place to the dynamic correlation between desire and world.

(2) This first, and properly phenomenological, level of analysis is doomed to be overcome. The question that emerges is indeed that of the status of the world that the subject of desire, or better the subject as desire, relates to. In truth, the dynamic characterization of the subject resonates with the characterization of the world, and the dynamic phenomenology opens the way for a cosmology, instead of an ontology. The question here is no other than that of the meaning of being of the world, insofar as it supports that of the subject, constitutes the ground of its characteristic dynamism, or once again of the community of being, of the ontological kinship between the poles of the correlation, between the desire and the world. It is here that, in light of the belonging that characterizes the subject, it is possible to effectuate a regressive move, that, from the meaning of the subject, leads to the meaning of the world in which the latter is inscribed. Indeed, if the mode of being of the subject is movement, and if the latter belongs to the world, i.e. it is made of the same stuff of it, then it has to be concluded that the world itself *exists in a dynamic mode*. The dynamic reality of the subject reveals the originally processual dimension of the world, and the movement of the subject proceeds in truth from this movement that makes the essence itself of the world. The desire, in its own dynamism, inherits from a movement already begun and that it only prolongs, that of the world. The subject does not begin the movement, but begins in the movement. This originary movement responds then to the question of the common being of the poles of the correlation, of the identity that sustains the phenomenalizing relation, and it is in that that ontology takes the face of a cosmology. I name this originary movement *proto-movement* [*archi-movement*] as long as it is the source of all dynamism, the move-

ment at work in every movement. But this proto-movement is equally *proto-life* [*archi-vie*] insofar as it is the movement at work in every life, the one from which every living being inherits. It only has to be added that that which holds for the subject holds for the movement from which it proceeds, given that the latter is not of a different nature from that of the subject. Therefore, the dynamic phenomenology, for which the subject exists as movement, leads to a *phenomenological dynamics* for which *every* movement, like that of the subject, is a phenomenalizing movement.

This result leads to two questions. On the one hand, what does the proto-movement consists in? On the other hand, in what sense can it be called phenomenalizing? The movement that characterizes the world cannot be a movement of which the world would be the subject, like an intra-wordly movement, but the movement through which the world makes itself a world, a movement of becoming-a-world [*mondification*]. The source of this movement must be something different from the world, that nonetheless is not a nothing, given that evidently what is at stake is not a creation. This movement proceeds from an undifferentiated background, and it is no other then than the process through which this background differentiates from itself in differentiating within itself, i.e. in producing differences from which the singular beings are born. What is at stake is a process of individuation through differentiation and thus delimitation, being understood that the background remains co-present in that which emerges from it, and that, as a consequence, its lack of determination persists within the determined. This comes to saying that no being is completely individuated. Thereby, the world in its most originary sense, is an ontogenetic power, power of giving birth to the beings within the background, power of producing multiplicity and, insofar as the world never stops transforming itself and remains on principle infinite, this power has the characteristic of being reborn from its products, it nourishes from that which it produces. This is the reason why I call it superpower [*surpuissance*]. So the process of the world, process of becoming-a-world, goes from the world to the world, from the worlding world [*monde mondifiant*], that is superpower, to the worlded world [*monde mondifié*], that is nothing but the provisory product of this superpower. It follows that three meanings of the world must be distinguished: the world as an undifferentiated background, which is at the same time its own power of determination, the world as an open multiplicity produced by that superpower, and lastly, the world as a sediment of the unity of the power within the multiple, i.e. as totality.

Now, the question is how to understand the sense in which this process draws upon the phenomenalization, and is thus a process of manifestation. The latter signifies an exiting or passing over the occultation, in such a way that the sense that one confers to the manifestation depends on the sense that one attributes to the occultation. There is a first form of being hidden: by being covered, by the interposition of a layer, be it or not the work of the subject. The manifestation consists then in a withdrawal of this layer, in an unveiling, and it is in this way that manifestation has been most often thought of. But there is a second way, more secrete and radical, of being hidden: through fusion with the surroundings, absence of delimitation or definition. The manifestation cannot consist then in nothing else but a detachment, the constitution of a boundary with the surrounding, in brief in a differentiation or a definition. Now, that is exactly the work of the world as we defined it: it delimits beings in differentiating them, it makes them come out from the undifferentiated background. Thereby, the condition of production of the being is also that of its appearing, so that the process of becoming-a-world is equally a process of phenomenalization, and the proto-movement is a proto-manifestation.

(3) The phenomenological dynamics leads thus to show an originary manifestation that merges with the process of becoming-a-world, an anonymous manifestation that is not given yet to anyone but is nonetheless susceptible of being gathered by every subject. The decisive point here is that phenomenality is disjoint from subjectivity. The former is the product of that which appears, and not of a consciousness that relates to it. It remains nonetheless as necessary to account for that which could be called the secondary appearing, the appearing to a subject. Insofar as the appearing is coextensive with being, this question is nothing other than one about the *genesis* of the subject himself. We thus have to double the regressive demarche that, on the basis of the belonging, led from the movement of the subject to that of the world, with a progressive demarche that reaches back from the world to the subject, from the originary phenomenality to the secondary appearing. Now, it follows from what has been said that the meaning of being of the subject is that of a *limitation*. Indeed, our movement is distinguished from that of the world by its powerlessness. It does not produce anything but desire, and it is because it cannot produce anything that it desires. This desire characterizes then a situation of ontological exile: the subject relates to the power of the world only in the mode of the loss, as if he found himself isolated from the movement of becoming-a-world, and were only joined to it under the form of an aspiration. In brief, dynamic phenomenology proceeds by negation from the phenomenological dynamics: everything happens as if the superpower of the world would negate itself, finishing itself, and would in this way fall outside of itself in the forms of a powerless movement, that desires for lack of being

able to produce. But there surely is a power to this powerlessness, that of making appear: cut off from the world, the subject only relates to it in the mode of desire, only grasps it *in absentia* and, by the same, makes it appear. Or better, the appearing as such is presence of that which remains absent, presence of that which is always evasive, and cannot thus be given but in the desire.

The question of the secondary appearing, i.e. the subject, merges then with that of the possibility of this limitation within the superpower of the world, from which proceeds the passage from the worldly process to the finite movement that characterizes us. Now, this limitation is, precisely, impossible and this passage as a consequence unthinkable, simply because this possibility is incompatible with the essence of the proto-movement of the world. Indeed, the falling outside of the world cannot be the work of the world: what is proper of the superpower is indeed that it is incapable of limiting itself, its productivity cannot mutate in powerlessness, the essence could not possibly be the source of its own negation. It has to be concluded that the scission that gives birth to the subject affects the world throughout but does not proceed from it in any way. The scission is without cause or reason within the world. That is the reason why it has to be understood as an event, a *proto-event* [*archi-evenement*] that alters the proto-movement of the world, while at the same time remaining foreign to it: movement within the movement, like a sort of metaphysical *clinamen*. The event has indeed the characteristic that it is without cause or reason within that which it affects. It is thus as such nothing determined, or better, its mode of being is that of a nothing, and, finally, it transforms throughout that which it achieves. In other words, one only apprehends itself through its effects. The fact of the subject merges with this proto-event, or, better, the subject is that which proceeds from it. He is the form in which the proto-movement of the world finds itself affected. I have named *metaphysics* the dimension opened by this proto-movement, not only to underline that it is foreign to the order of the essence, i.e. of the proto-movement, but also in reference to the metaphysics, in a sense very special, that Husserl claimed in order to designate the proto-facticity of the subject, a metaphysics that is in the antipodes of an investigation about causes and reasons.

These are my main contributions in the field of phenomenology. They could be summarized in three points. First of all, I tried to show *the a priori of the a priori* of the correlation between the transcendent world and the subject, and I showed that this first a priori is *double*. On the one hand, it is cosmologic, insofar as the relation presupposes a belonging of the subject and thus a common ground, that I defined as proto-movement. On the other hand, it is metaphysic because the relation presupposes a difference, a separation of the subject *vis-à-vis* the world.

This separation, far from being able to proceed from the world, draws on a pure event that, beyond the movement, is the most radical figure of negativity. Thereby, phenomenology only accomplishes itself truly in a sort of overtaking of itself within itself, in the form of a cosmology and a metaphysics, overtaking in and through which it does not become what is other from it, but rejoins its own foundation. Secondly, far from being the very place of reason, the subject is the without-reason [*sans raison*] par excellence, that of which one cannot give reason because it refers to an ontological weakness of the world of which the subject cannot be the source. Finally, my perspective arrives at giving to finitude a radical status because my perspective consists in thinking the human being starting from finitude as metaphysical event instead of thinking the finitude starting from the human being under the title of anthropological predicate, as it had been thought before. Finitude is not an attribute but the event that comes to weaken the power of the proto-life, or shatter the plenitude of the world: the human being, like all living beings, is born from this event. Finitude is thus not a limitation in our power to make the world appear, an incapacity of our subjectivity, but on the contrary its unique and fundamental condition. It is not a weakness of subjectivity but the metaphysical weakness from which this subjectivity is born.

3. What is the proper role of phenomenology in relation to other disciplines?

It seems to me that the role of phenomenology with respect to other disciplines is mainly critical. In fact, the majority of disciplines work within the framework of a spontaneous ontology that is most often naively realist or naturalist. Thereby, sciences are in general lead to consider that the concepts and laws that they bring out characterize the very being of their object, in brief, that they have an ontological scope. The role of phenomenology is thus the one that Husserl granted to it already in *Krisis*: reducing this pseudo-evidence in order to show the phenomenal ground upon which science works, a ground with respect to which the constructions of science can appear as what they are, namely an ideal superstructure, a clothing of ideas. Likewise, theoretical biology believes to describe the essence of the living being, when what it really does is bringing out the physico-chemical conditions of the latter. Now, in order to start working, it needs to be able to have its object given, i.e. recognize the living being as such, which cannot be but the accomplishment of another living being. It is starting from this originary experience that the notions of living being and life are susceptible of being clarified; *vis-à-vis* this layer of originary experience, the concepts of biology can only appear as abstract and derived categories. This critical demarche that, coming back to the mode of originary giveness of the object, aims at being foundational can be repeated in every field of knowledge, including in particular the field of human sciences.

4. What have been the most significant advances in phenomenology?

It seems to me that that which has been done in phenomenology represents an advance with respect to the thought of the founders, and that it is difficult to establish a hierarchy in this respect.

5. What are the most important open problems in phenomenology and what are the prospects for progress?

Each current in phenomenology, and there are numerous, opens up a field of specific problems, in virtue of its own advances. The richness and fecundity of what is done in every direction should be underlined. For my part, I would say that, along a line that seems to me is historic phenomenology, the difficulty is to avoid every form of ingenuous realism, following the foundational inspiration of phenomenology according to which the meaning of being of being is its appearing, without however falling into a subjectivism, that persists even where it is expressly denounced, as it is the case in Heidegger. How to think then the appearing without making it rest on a subject? How to think the appearing as appearing of the world in the double meaning of the genitive, i.e. as that which gives the world and, at the same time, as that of which the world is subject? On the response to this question depends the possibility of authentically thinking the phenomenal world, but also subjectivity, the body and, finally, intersubjectivity.

2

Rudolf Bernet

Professor emeritus and President of the Husserl Archives
KU Leuven (Belgium)

---

1. Why were you initially drawn to phenomenology?
When I began studying philosophy in Louvain in 1964 I was almost automatically "drawn to phenomenology". It was then a major philosophical orientation, and it had the most inspiring teachers in Louvain. What especially attracted me to phenomenology were the concrete analyses of human existence in a language that reminded me more of literature than of traditional philosophical concepts such as those my former teachers in Switzerland had been using without ever questioning their meaning. I had initially considered studying art history. It is no wonder then that I immediately fell under the spell of Merleau-Ponty and Heidegger when I came to Louvain.

Phenomenology also attracted me by its fresh approach to the history of philosophy. Already in my first year in Louvain I became acquainted with Husserl's presentation of Galileo, Heidegger's interpretation of Kant, Aristotle, and the pre-Socratics, and with Merleau-Ponty's texts on Marxism. It was as if I understood for the first time and could follow step by step the development of a philosophical argument while reading a text. It was all marvelous, and I decided to go on with philosophy as long as I could–instead of turning to the study of something more serious, as my well-meaning parents had wished.

The first idea of a topic for my personal research was to work on a phenomenological interpretation of Leibniz. With Merleau-Ponty in the back of my mind, I began studying Leibniz's monadological theory of perception and his conception of space. A monograph by Dietrich Mahnke, a student of Husserl's, first made me aware of a possible Husserlian approach to Leibniz. An older friend of mine working at the Husserl Archives, Iso Kern, then suggested that I should first become better acquainted with Husserl. Iso Kern, Rudolf Boehm and the writings of Eugen Fink became my chief mentors in my early study of Husserl. I became a Husserl scholar almost by chance, however I remain deeply indebted to him–more than to any other philosopher. I felt and still feel attracted by the flexibility and creativity of his thought, and also by his concern for conceptual rigor. However, I began soon, with the help of Heidegger, Levinas, and Derrida, to question the metaphysical presuppositions of Husserl's phenomenology.

After having studied in Heidelberg for one year I was, in 1968, offered my first job in Louvain as a teaching assistant of my most inspiring phenomenological teacher, Jacques Taminiaux. Two years later I got a full-time position as research assistant and editor at the Husserl Archives, then directed by Father Van Breda. After my PhD (1976) I became associate professor (1983), full professor (1988), and professor emeritus (2011) at KU Leuven. Phenomenology became so much a part of my thinking and life that a more appropriate formulation of this question would have been: what has, at least partially, drawn you *out* of phenomenology? It was not, as one might suspect, psychoanalysis; it was rather a growing interest in phenomena the meaning of which does not essentially depend on human experience. Deleuze played an important role in this, and his work introduced me to Nietzsche, Bergson, and Spinoza.

2. What are your main contributions to the field of phenomenology?

I don't think this is up to me to say. I am also reluctant to draw a final picture of what I have experienced as a series of philosophical investigations with little preconceived plan and no final result. Of course, my list of publications and what I have achieved as a teacher, editor, and director of the Husserl Archives can count as a contribution. But it doesn't make me blind to the modesty of my contribution to a renewal of philosophical thought. And how should I account for my "contributions to the field of phenomenology"? Should I refer to the objective results (the 'work' done or *opus*) and their reception or to the experiences of joy and of misfortune in my intellectual life? There is a phenomenology of inner life, and there is a hermeneutical phenomenology–also in the account of one's own contribution to phenomenology.

In my *philosophical* development I have become progressively dissatisfied with a merely static phenomenological analysis of intentional correlations between subject and object, and increasingly sensitive to the dynamism of mental and bodily processes, as well as of natural forces. This is how questions of temporality and, later, questions concerning driving impulses, passive affections and desires have moved into the foreground of my interests. Much of my work in this field consists in the exploration of historical positions: from Aristotle to Husserl and Freud, via Leibniz, Schopenhauer and Nietzsche. These historic and systematic investigations have had an important impact on my phenomenological views on both consciousness and subjectivity. I have attempted to enlarge these key notions sufficiently to make room for the mental and bodily phenomena evinced by psychoanalysis and psychiatry. Unwilling to completely give up a phenomenology of consciousness and human subjectivity I have stretched their meaning as much as conceptual coherence allowed. The same can be said of my work in the field of a phenomenological esthetics and anthropology. By temperament and by conviction I have always avoided becoming involved in some orthodoxy or in polemical exclusions.

In addition to my work on the phenomena uncovered by others, did I myself discover any new phenomenologically relevant phenomena? Maybe my description and conceptualization of a subject's fluctuation between annihilation and self-affirmation–as observed in experiences of personal traumatism–could count as such. In some of my more recent work on the feelings of home-sickness and nostalgia, on suffering and psychotic delusions (also in artistic representations) one can find attempts to combine the analysis of mental processes with the description of forms of expressive bodily behavior. Which new phenomenological perspectives are opened by my most recent work on Spinoza remains to be seen.

My *academic* contributions to phenomenology have benefitted from the most favorable institutional and personal circumstances. My understanding of Husserl and Heidegger, of Merleau-Ponty and Sartre, of Levinas and Derrida, of Gadamer and Cassirer owe much to my colleagues and students. My editions of Husserl's texts on time-consciousness and my former editorship of *Husserliana* and *Phaenomenologica* are only a small contribution to what the Husserl Archives in Leuven have done for phenomenology in their now more than 75 years of existence.

3. What is the proper role of phenomenology in relation to other disciplines?

Is phenomenology a philosophical "discipline" and what kind of "discipline" is philosophy? A scientific discipline has a real material object; phenomenological philosophy is a mode or style of thinking about phenomena taken as mere possibilities. What a (transcendental or eidetic) phenomenology of intentional consciousness has in common with all phenomenologies of life, of human existence, of bodily behavior, of linguistic expression, of social action, of scientific research and artistic creation is a distinctive approach to the phenomena, as well as their description and conceptualization.

There is no phenomenology without (some kind of) *phenomenological reduction*. Negatively put, the phenomenological reduction consists in a suspension of all beliefs and certainties belonging to natural life and in a questioning of its prejudices and presuppositions. It is about a change of attitude and not a loss or destruction of the world. This negative operation of the phenomenological reduction allows for the positive and constructive work of letting things show from themselves as they truly are in themselves, i.e. as pure phenomenological phenomena. Familiar things appear in a new light: in their true mode of being and in a new perspective that makes visible formerly invisible phenomena. Natural things become, as Husserl says, an 'index' for the inquiry into how they are given to experience. Questioning the presuppositions of natural life and opening the possibility of another view on the world also radically changes the meaning of all the scientific "disciplines" that are built on the natural attitude. In its exploration of the appearing of things for an experiencing subject, the role of the phenomenological reduction is thus both critical and revealing.

The phenomenological reduction acquires a particular significance for all *sciences* (including phenomenology) when it reduces ephemeral phenomenological phenomena to their essential and necessary features. This is what an *eidetic reduction* achieves. An eidetic phenomenology is less a science of abstract formal essences than of what Spinoza calls "common notions", i.e. of what diverse concrete phenomena have essentially in common. It allows for the elaboration of concrete or, as Husserl says, "material" phenomenological ontologies. Husserl's main interest was in the elaboration of a material ontology of the mind and of its phenomenological mode of experience. Needless to say, such a "pure phenomenological psychology" is of the greatest relevance for all sciences dealing with human mental processes: empirical and cognitive psychology, psychopathology, science of religion, esthetics, etc. Husserl's program of a material ontology of psycho-physical human behavior has been further developed by subsequent generations of phenomenologists, especially in the field of a phenomenological sociology and a phenomenology of cultural life. While naïve material ontologies often endorse the objectivistic and naturalistic prejudices of natural life and science, phenomenologically-transformed material ontologies involve a radical departure from all object-oriented sciences. Introducing the consideration of the experiencing human subject into all scientific investigations, eidetic phenomenology contributes to a humanization of the sciences without falling prey to psychologism or relativistic worldviews.

However, for Husserl it is only with the *transcendental reduction* that phenomenology reaches its full potential for a reformation of natural life and the sciences. On his view on the transcendental reduction, the meaning of being of everything is re-conducted to and derived from an egological, transcendentally-constitutive consciousness. Later phenomenologists have developed alternative versions of a transcendental phenomenology: without ego, without consciousness, and even without subjective constitution. They have also claimed that the perspective of a transcendentally constituting theoretical subject is too narrow to account for the different modes of the being (real/unreal, possible/impossible, necessary/contingent, etc.) of all beings. New proposals for a phenomenological *philosophia prima* have emerged–even claiming the status of first philosophy for ethics (Levinas).

In all its forms, however, it is "the proper role of phenomenology" to become a true "discipline" of *philosophy*. This has always been the ambition of phenomenology since Husserl's "Ideas pertaining to a pure phenomenology and phenomenological philosophy". What a philosopher thinks relates to the basis of all human endeavors, to their "conditions of possibility". What phenomenology adds to a traditional mode of philosophical thinking is the effort to check the revealing force of its concepts against the truth of the phenomenological (and not the natural) phenomena. Whether philosophical thinking can reach a stable or even absolute ground depends, for the phenomenologist, on the phenomena and not on the radicalism of human will.

4. What have been the most significant advances in phenomenology?

My first answer is, without any hesitation: *a new mode of philosophical thinking*. What counts as new largely depends on what one takes the former modes to be. Phenomenology is an alternative to both positivism and speculative idealism. But it shares with positivism and empiricism the recourse to experience (or to "the phenomena themselves") as the final criterion for the validity of all philosophical affirmations. It also shares with speculative idealism the ambition of thinking the phenomena rather than merely describing them.

As to the *fields* where the most significant advances of and in phenomenology have been accomplished, one should be more hesitant. It is probably not philosophy of language, a field in which phenomenology seems far from having developed its full potential. Neither is it, for the same reason, philosophy of science or philosophy of nature. In *philosophical aesthetics* phenomenology–occasionally associated with hermeneutics or deconstructivism–has done better. As a science of pure phenomena phenomenology has a particular affinity with painting. As a science of phenomena that are treated as mere possibilities phenomenology also has much in common with creative artistic imagination, especially with literature. As a science of inner time-consciousness phenomenology has a privileged access to musical experience, to different kinds of memory, and to phenomena related to history and narration. As a science of empathy and values phenomenology has also become a significant voice in the field of social sciences, cultural studies, ethics, politics, and philosophy of religion. In all these domains phenomenologists, beginning with Husserl himself, have made a significant impact beyond philosophical circles.

However, all this remains rooted in a phenomenological *philosophy of mind*: the core business of phenomenology. It is for its renewed account of perception, imagination, memory, and time-consciousness that phenomenology is best known. Ethics and social sciences have also much benefited from a phenomenological analysis of *empathy* and *feelings for values*, of *will* and *action*. In cultural studies, politics and history of religion the phenomenological analysis of *intersubjectivity* and *historical transmission*, of the sedimentation of subjective mental processes and the creation of symbolic institutions, of situations of crisis and the possibility of renewal has set new accents.

When it comes to the most significant advances *inside* of phenomenology, it is likely that one will immediately mention its theory of the *perception* of things and space. In phenomenology the experience and organization of the perceiving body and of bodily movements have gradually received all the attention they deserve. What began as a representational theory of perception has progressively made room for the study of subjective *embodiment* and bodily enactment. This subsequently allowed phenomenology to turn to the study of all kinds of non-perceptual *symbolic bodily comportments*. The new analysis of expressive bodily comportments has also led to a better account of all forms of *intersubjectivity* and social life that cannot be reduced to mental processes of empathy.

For many phenomenologists (including myself) the extension of the meaning of '*consciousness*' and of '*subjectivity*' also counts as a significant advance in phenomenology. Phenomenologists have carefully investigated presentifying modes of intentionality such as memory, imagination and empathy that owe only little to objective perception. They have also complemented their study of intentional consciousness with an investigation of all kinds of inner sensations and emotions. Almost all of them were particularly attentive to the status of pre-reflexive consciousness, degrees of awareness and intensities of affections. This led phenomenologists to reformulate the meaning of human subjectivity, to distinguish between ego and self, and to emphasize the embeddedness of human life in mundane situations and social institutions.

However, none of these advances would have been possible without the discovery and study of the multifaceted phenomenon of a subjective *passivity*. Passivity is the key concept in all phenomenologies that focus on the genesis of consciousness and subjectivity in the context of knowledge, ethics, aesthetics or religion. Phenomenology has given an entirely new meaning to passivity–and conjointly to activity and activity in passivity. When subjectivity is no longer equivalent with spontaneity and self-determination, then the nature of human freedom and responsibility also appears in a new light. As a consequence, new concepts have emerged in phenomenology, such as an insistent external command or call and a free subjective response or responsive responsibility.

5. What are the most important open problems in phenomenology and what are the prospects for progress?

In my opinion the most important open problem is the *relation of phenomenology to metaphysics and ontology*. This problem has remained open, at least partially, because phenomenologists have remained fixated on the disagreement between Husserl and Heidegger. One can agree with Heidegger's claim that there is no philosophy of knowledge (and even no philosophy at all) without metaphysics, while still disagreeing with his description of traditional metaphysics as an onto-theo-logy of presence. One can also be dissatisfied with the formalism of Heidegger's later meditations on being and still claim that a philosopher's choice between the analogous, univocal or equivocal meaning of being remains of fundamental importance. The analysis of the relation and difference between human and animal life, between oneself and other human beings, between cognition and affectivity, between the one and the many all depend on this formal choice. Closely linked to this is the philosopher's choice for a philosophy of transcendence or immanence. In the course of the history of phenomenology all possible choices have been explored. Is this so because of the diversity of phenomenologists, or because of the diversity of the phenomena? Can the phenomena impose a metaphysical choice or does the way phenomena appear and have meaning depend on a previous metaphysical choice? Phenomenologists need to think more about *philosophia prima*–not instead of the analysis of concrete phenomena but through it.

Thinking about being or the most fundamental structures underlying all experience by means of a descriptive analysis of different kinds of phenomena must also make phenomenologists aware of further categorical and conceptual issues. Heidegger's deconstruction of the traditional metaphysics of presence, substance, and subjectivity has been too general and too exclusive to be of great help for a phenomenologist who wonders about the application of conventional categories to (new) phenomena. When pondering, for example, the advantages and disadvantages of accounting for the phenomena belonging to a particular biological species in terms of substance, function or process, the phenomenologist is in need of a broad metaphysical background, and of a genuine flexibility in its use.

In thinking more about categories, phenomenologists should also reconsider which categories must, in principle, be banned from an analysis of *human existence*. Is it Substance? Essence? Necessity? Causality? Is everything in human existence then a matter of heteronomy, of facticity, of contingent possibilities, of motivation and choice? Among all the concepts used in a phenomenological analysis of human existence, there is one that clearly sticks out: *freedom*. Phenomenological existentialists have all enthusiastically pleaded in favor of the freedom to shape the meaning of one's own life by an active projection into the future. Their plea has been successful because it seemed to be the only conceivable alternative to a mechanistic form of determinism. But contemporary science and contemporary social life raise new challenges and require new philosophical meditations on the nature of human freedom.

Phenomenology is also still in need of a clarification of its use of the concept of *'life'* and of its relation to diverse forms of a metaphysical *vitalism*. Phenomenologists, including Husserl and Heidegger, have made a too-indiscriminate use of life-related concepts. Other phenomenologists have fallen prey to a naïve form of vitalism. The greatest danger of traditional philosophies of life for phenomenology is not their pretended irrationalism, but their belief in order and progress, in first origins and final ends. Phenomenologists should not forget about all that is negative in the development of life: events of interruption, dissociation, misfortune and catastrophe. They also need to think more about their position in the traditional debate between spiritual and materialistic forms of a metaphysical vitalism.

Some people complain that contemporary phenomenology has become *too academic*. They probably mean: too preoccupied with its own historical development and too little sensitive to the new challenges in our contemporary life-world. On their view, phenomenologists should be more present in contemporary debates about nationalism and migration, about territories and globalization, about the new media, about the decline of democracy, about race and gender, etc. Phenomenologists need, however, to remain phenomenologists. It is the main task of a contemporary phenomenology to revise and reshape traditional concepts and theories in the light of an unprejudiced description of the new phenomena appearing in the changed situation of the present world.

All my wishes relate to a better *balance between innovative descriptions of phenomena and conceptual rigor* in the work of phenomenologists. Taking much of its inspiration from science, arts and religion, phenomenology cannot compete with them on their own ground. It must compete with conceptually strong schools in contemporary philosophy. Doing justice to the richness and diversity of our experience of phenomena in the appropriate form of a non-formal conceptual thinking has always stood at the center of Husserl's phenomenological program. This is how he was lead into the investigation of the *formation* of concepts on the basis of pre-predicative and predominantly passive experiences. Phenomenology needs new, creative thinkers who, like Husserl, do not surrender judgment to mere experience and faithful description of experience to mere conceptual argumentation.

However, the biggest challenge for phenomenology is, and has always been, to conceptually account for the phenomena the meaning of which does not essentially depend on human experience. For these phenomena Husserl's dismissal of a phenomenology of a being-in-itself (*Sein an sich*) and his phenomenological idealism become utterly problematic. And his sketch of an analysis of the significance of the basic phenomenon of the Earth gains renewed relevance. Phenomenologists must learn to see and respect what, in the phenomena, resists the inquisitive observation and the bestowal of meaning by an intentional consciousness. Many of their "things-themselves" have a being and a life of their own that, without therefore falling outside of all human experience, do not lend themselves to a straightforward phenomenological grasp.

3

John B. Brough

Professor Emeritus, Philosophy
Georgetown University (U.S.A.)

---

1. Why were you initially drawn to phenomenology?

A pair of statements I came upon not long after I began to study Husserl capture why I was first drawn to phenomenology. They remain touchstones for me. One is from Simone de Beauvoir's *The Prime of Life*. Raymond Aron, de Beauvoir reports, had been in Berlin studying Husserl, about whom Sartre knew very little at the time. Back in Paris, Aron joined Sartre and de Beauvoir at a café for apricot cocktails. The talk turned to Husserl. Pointing to his glass, Aron said: "'You see, my dear fellow, if you are a phenomenologist, you can talk about this cocktail and make philosophy out of it!' Sartre turned pale with emotion at this. Here was just the thing he had been longing to achieve for years–to describe objects just as he saw and touched them and extract philosophy from the process"[1]. The other statement comes from Aron Gurwitsch: "In the second of his *Meditations on the First Philosophy*, Descartes had established the privilege of consciousness as the only and universal medium of access to whatever exists. Husserl has renewed and reaffirmed this Cartesian discovery"[2].

As an undergraduate majoring in philosophy, I developed an interest in Descartes and Sartre. My knowledge of the two was hardly profound, but each did something that seemed to me to be philosophically important. In Descartes's case, I was struck by the clarity and orderly movement of his thought as it progressed from one meditation to the next, and especially from his own existence as a mind or thinking substance to the world. It impressed me as well that he offered a method that he claimed could be put to work cultivating the tree of knowledge from root to branch. Sartre offered a contrast to Descartes, but also a similarity. The contrast was in the sorts of experience Sartre brought under philosophical scrutiny–

---

[1] Simone de Beauvoir, *The Prime of Life*, Cleveland and New York: The World Publishing Company, 1962, p. 112.

[2] Aron Gurwitsch, *Studies in Phenomenology and Psychology*, Evanston: Northwestern University Press, 1966, p. xix.

sincerity, lying, bad faith, "the look," which were not at all the kinds of phenomena that appeared in Descartes, although they certainly appeared in life. But there was also a "logic" and a dualism at work in Sartre, if not between a mind conceived as a substance (which was anathema to Sartre) and the world, then between human consciousness, Sartre's "for-itself," and all that was not human consciousness, the "in-itself." Intentionality, the Husserlian position that consciousness is always the consciousness of something, played a key role in Sartre's thought, but my understanding of it at this point was sketchy at best.

Beyond studying Sartre in an elementary way, I was not exposed to phenomenology as an undergraduate in any formal sense, and certainly not to Husserl. Early in graduate school, however, I was introduced to Merleau-Ponty. Though I had admired Descartes's clarity, I had never been persuaded by his ontology, especially by his dualism. Merleau-Ponty helped me understand why. Although Descartes's view of mind and body may have posed insurmountable problems about how such radically different kinds of being could interact, and may have made a puzzle of sensory experience, the real difficulty with his thought, I came to think, was that his position could not give a satisfactory account of experience as we live it. This was equally true of the classical empiricists. Merleau-Ponty, on the other hand, focused precisely on that experience. He sought to understand it on its own terms, breaking with Cartesian dualism and empiricism alike. Furthermore, he explored some of the same sorts of experience that Sartre did, but not with Sartre's dualism of for-itself and in-itself, which, despite the brilliance and depth of Sartre's descriptions of phenomena, compelled him by a kind of perverse logic to conclude that the self is "nothing," that sincerity and love are impossible, and that hell is other people. I would not have formulated it this way at the time, but I realized that Sartre forced the phenomena to submit to the logic of his own dualism. Although I still had not studied Husserl at this point, I must have had some inkling of his ideal of "presuppositionless philosophy."

The exposure to Merleau-Ponty was important for me because it revealed ways of doing philosophy without following in Descartes's footsteps or in those of the atomistic empiricists. Merleau-Ponty also helped to wean me away from my undergraduate view of philosophy as a gallery of dazzling conceptual constructions. It set me on a path of philosophy understood, not as a set of arguments proving or failing to prove this or that, but as a careful investigation of the fundamental structures of our experience. It let me see that philosophy can and should go back "to the things themselves," though I had not yet heard that phrase.

While I knew that Merleau-Ponty's liberating approach was phenomenological in some sense, I did not yet have a firm understanding of what phenomenology, particularly in the full Husserlian sense, was. Put differently, I did not fully appreciate the fact that it was really phenomenology that I found liberating.

It was only later in graduate school that I began to study Husserl seriously. It was then that I started to develop a deeper sense of the significance of intentionality and could appreciate Aron Gurwitsch's remark that intentionality is the universal medium of access to whatever exists. Husserl's conception of intentionality and phenomenology offered an alternative to the closed sphere of the Cartesian mind: a subject that transcends itself toward objects. It established the possibility, raised by Raymond Aron in his conversation with Sartre, of bringing everything that occurs in the vast range of human experience under the philosopher's gaze. This revelation of what a philosophy properly conceived could do turned me into an unapologetic, though hopefully not a narrow-minded, "Husserlian phenomenologist."

2. What are your main contributions to the field of phenomenology?

I have tried to contribute to phenomenology mainly in three ways: through translations of Husserl's texts; through analyses of the phenomenology of time and time-consciousness; and through reflections on Husserl's conception of image-consciousness, including its connections to art, with an emphasis on the nature and role of images in contemporary and modern art, in photography, and in film.

Let me first say a word about translating. I have translated two volumes in the Husserliana series–Husserliana X (on time-consciousness) and Husserliana XXIII (on phantasy, image-consciousness, and memory)– and am currently finishing a translation of volume VIII in the Materialien series (Husserl's late texts on time-constitution). All have appeared or will appear in the "Collected Works" series of English translations of Husserl's works. Translating Husserl is a time-consuming, difficult, and often perilous activity. For one thing, while Husserl can be a model of clarity, as he is in his discussion of image-consciousness, he can also be fiendishly difficult, which is the rule when he explores the murky depths of time-consciousness. Vocabulary questions regularly accompany the conceptual obscurities, since Husserl is quite willing to coin terms and to use established terms in his own fashion. Translating such texts confirms with a vengeance the old adage that translation is always interpretation. The interpreting can even demand–distressingly for the translator–a considerable degree of invention. No translator can run the gamut of Husserl's texts and emerge unscathed.

One might ask, then, why bother translating? What is the motivation? Well, translating Husserl is a challenge, and challenges can be exciting. But one needs a more serious motivation than that. When I have become interested in translating something by Husserl, it is after I have spent a considerable time studying and writing about it, and, of most importance, have found it to be particularly fruitful philosophically. At some point, it just strikes me that the text should be available in English. Husserl's writings on time-consciousness, for example, are unmatched in the philosophical literature as investigations of the *experience* of time, including the various forms of memory, expectation, and perception, and of the ways in which time-consciousness weaves our lives together. Husserl's later reflections on time, in Materialen VIII, cover a broad array of phenomena, among them the Ego's relation to temporality; the notion of the "living present" at the center of conscious experience; the "temporalizing" of the self, the world, and other egos; sleep, waking, and death; and the constitution with others of communal space, time, and world. As perplexing as many of these late texts often are, they nonetheless offer Husserl's final, and in many cases new and important, reflections on topics that he had pursued for decades. Their availability in translation will hopefully prove useful for the further exploration of the issues he discusses.

There is another reason why translating is important. Husserl was a prolific writer, but not a prolific publisher. Much of what appeared during his lifetime was concerned with laying out the nature of phenomenology and establishing its status as a new and "rigorous science." These published "introductions" to phenomenology can be abstract, and they sometimes contain formulations of basic themes, such as the phenomenological reduction, that invite misinterpretation. In many of his posthumous writings, however, one gets a much better sense of what phenomenology is and what its practice involves. One sees Husserl actually *doing* phenomenological work. He does not just talk about the phenomenological method in such texts; he uses it, reaching insight after insight. Translation gives a larger audience access to these texts. Most of the translations in the "Collected Works" series also include substantial translator's prefaces intended to introduce the reader to the content of the work and to stitch together what is often a fragmented collection of notes, sketches, and lecture manuscripts.

Finally, translating is a way of entering as intimately as possible into a philosopher's thought. That's the selfish side of translating. A good translation, however, also aims at helping the reader make the same journey.

The second area to which I have tried to contribute is the phenomenology of time and time-consciousness, particularly in Husserl. I have already noted that Husserl's account of our awareness of time is the most thorough in the history of philosophy. Husserl wrote that time-consciousness is a "wonder" and the most difficult of all phenomenological problems (it is no surprise that he cites Augustine's famous remark that our confident assumption that we know what time is evaporates the moment someone asks us to explain it). He adds, however, that it is also perhaps the most important matter in the whole of phenomenology–"most important" because it investigates the very ground and possibility of consciousness and its objects.

If time-consciousness is a wonder, Husserl's phenomenology of time-consciousness is equally so. It offers a model of how phenomenology can set forth the distinctions and differences that abound in a fundamental area of our experience. Given the richness of Husserl's account of time-consciousness and the limitations of an interview such as this, I will discuss only what I have come to see as the most salient features of his view.

I still recall the force with which Husserl's distinction between retention and ordinary memory struck me when I first encountered it decades ago. Retention, which Husserl sometimes called "primary" memory, and its sibling, protention, are the forms of consciousness making us aware of what is just past and of what is just coming. These are primordial moments that, together with primal impression understood as the experience of the now, first make possible the consciousness of temporal unities running off in time. An act that I experience–a perception, for example–begins, lasts for a while, and then flows away, to be replaced by another act. The same is true of its object. To be conscious of time and temporal objects therefore means to be conscious of more than the now. The indispensable thing that retention and protention do is to enable me to reach out beyond the now and be conscious of the immediate past and future, and thus to experience temporal objects and to preserve them in ever-changing temporal modes as they flow away.

Ordinary or "secondary" memory, of course, also lets me be conscious of the past, but it intends the more distant past, in the sense that it returns to an experience that I have already had and runs through it once again. In ordinary memory, therefore, I am conscious of an act that I have already constituted, while retention is a moment in the generative constitution of a new experience. Memory "re-collects," while retention "collects," that is, along with protention and primal impression, is the source of the original constitution of what is re-collected later. Thanks to retention and protention, I am not locked up in the now; I transcend it, and with that transcending the landscape of time begins to unfold for me. Ordinary memory and expectation can then fill out the rich and complex contours of a life lived in time.

Retention not only reaches out beyond the now and preserves or holds on to temporal objects as they elapse; it also modifies them. Preservation and modification form an inseparable pair in temporal experience.

If preserving an elapsed phase of a temporal object simply meant keeping it in consciousness as now, we would not have transcended the now at all. We would have no sense of the temporal flow or of temporal objects. What is preserved must be preserved as just *past*, not as still now, or, in protention, be intended as still to come. Only through modification of what I have preserved can I see a bird in flight or hear a melody rather than a jumble of simultaneous sounds. In making these observations, Husserl shows that we are always conscious of presence *and* absence. Husserlian phenomenology is no "metaphysics of presence."

All of this may seem self-evident. But it appears that way because Husserl's phenomenological analysis has let us *see* it. That is the remarkable thing about phenomenology: it gives us new eyes with which to see phenomena and uncover their wonders. It does not create a substitute universe; instead, it shines new light on the ordinary universe that has been there all along.

I have stressed the bond between preservation (and anticipation) and modification because it is fundamental to time-consciousness, and therefore to the three "levels" Husserl says are involved in time-constitution. In several essays I have attempted to show that Husserl's distinction between levels or dimensions of time-consciousness is central to his thought about time from 1911 or so until the end of his life. If I have made a contribution to the study of Husserl's phenomenology of time-consciousness, it would probably be here. In one respect, Husserl's talk about levels represents an effort to present in a concise way all that is involved in our awareness of time, and, ultimately, of ourselves. Thus Husserl distinguishes, first, the level of temporal objects–melodies, houses, and so on–intended by conscious acts; second, the level of acts and sensory contents, which are themselves temporal "objects," though not transcendent to consciousness; and third, "the absolute time-constituting flow of consciousness."

What precisely is the absolute flow, the third level noted above, and what does it constitute and how does it constitute it? Since acts of consciousness on the second level are themselves immanent temporal objects, that is, occur in immanent time, and since we are aware of them in a non-objective, pre-reflective way, Husserl claims that these acts must themselves be constituted in time-consciousness. This occurs through the absolute flow, which, in each of its phases, has retentional, impressional, and protentional moments that, together, constitute the consciousness of the act as a temporal unity, anticipating, presenting, preserving, and modifying its phases as they flow away. With this constitution of an intentional act, an act of perceiving a house, for example, what is perceived becomes constituted as a transcendent temporal object on the first level in Husserl's scheme. Husserl manages to explain in this way the constitution of both transcendent and immanent temporal objects, of acts and what they intend. It is important to realize that the absolute flow does not *perceive* the act as if it were an object like a house. Rather, the flow is the pre-objectifying consciousness of the act I am living through. Acts are only "perceived" in reflection.

The absolute consciousness is also responsible for a further achievement, one that particularly justifies the flow's description as "absolute". Through its retentional and protentional moments, the flow constitutes its own unity. The flow therefore possesses a "double intentionality," as Husserl puts it. It at once constitutes both itself as a flowing unity and the myriad of acts in the immanent time of level two. I am conscious that I am perceiving a house, but I also have some primitive awareness that my consciousness, my "absolute subjectivity," is ongoing and all-embracing, that my conscious life is not exhausted by this or that fleeting act, but that it endures as a perpetual source of new experience. To refer to the absolute flow as a "level" should not be construed to mean that it is separate or separable from what it constitutes and that it exists or could exist on its own. Husserl's point, I have argued, is that consciousness is a unity with constituting and constituted dimensions that are distinct but inseparable. There is no flow without the acts of which it is aware, and there are no acts without the flow that is aware of them.

There have been some lively debates about whether Husserl actually does distinguish between two levels *within* consciousness, as my account above presumes (the consensus now seems to be that he does) and whether the notion of an absolute flow distinct but inseparable from the level of acts is philosophically defensible (no consensus there). I have argued in various ways that Husserl's claims about the absolute flow can indeed be defended, but I freely grant that the difficulty and obscurity enveloping the notion of the flow – the "murky depths" I mentioned earlier – supply plenty of ground for continuing discussion. One hopes that further reflection will shed new light on this ultimate ground of self- and world-constitution, which I take to be what Husserl was attempting to explore with his notion of an "absolute" level of conscious life.

The third area in which I hope to have made some contribution is in the phenomenology of image-consciousness, including its relevance for the phenomenology of art. Husserl had little to say directly about art in his published works, although core ideas of his thought, such as intentionality, have proved to be highly effective instruments in the hands of phenomenological aestheticians such as Roman Ingarden and Mikel Dufrenne. In posthumously published texts concerned with images and image-consciousness, however, Husserl has some very interesting things to say about art and aesthetic experience, which is why, as I mentioned, I translated Husserliana Volume XXIII, in which the bulk of these texts appear. But one does not find a full-blown aesthetics in these texts. They do, however, leave a rich legacy of possibilities for the philosopher interested in the experience of art.

Husserl's account of image-consciousness is yet another example of how phenomenology can illuminate a vital area of human experience. Indeed, Husserl here manages to let us see clearly not only the essential structure of our awareness of images but of perception and phantasy as well. Perception, Husserl observes, has a single object: what is perceived, a building, say. Image-consciousness, on the other hand, involves three objects. When I look at a photograph of a building, an image stands before me as present and as there itself; I see it and in it I see a building. Husserl frequently calls this the "image-object." I am also aware that this image-object has a physical support, the paper on which the photograph is printed. This physical substratum is also an object, Husserl says, though when I perceive the image, my consciousness of its support is suppressed, although not altogether, since I am aware of a conflict between the image and its support. This conflict lets me experience the image as a fiction, a semblance, and not as a real thing given to me in ordinary perception. It is thanks to its physical support, which is a indeed something real in actual space and time, that the photographic image can hang on the wall in my room. What is represented in the photograph – the Flatiron Building in New York, for example –does not hang on the wall in my room. In that conflicting play of image and support, I am aware that I am conscious of an image and not actually perceiving a real thing.

There is still another "object" involved in image-consciousness: the *subject* of the image, in this case, the Flatiron Building. Here I experience another conflict. The image-building is only about 10 inches high and appears in shades of grey. The Flatiron Building itself is several stories high, and its facade displays a variety of colors, few of which are grey. The awareness of this difference again ensures that I experience an image and not a real thing. The image, of course, to borrow an idea from Arthur Danto, is "about" something; that is, it is about its subject, which one can see in the image. The Flatiron Building itself is not "about" anything in that sense.

Husserl concludes that the image, because it is not a real thing in the real world, is "nothing," a "nullity" or fiction. But it is a very odd kind of nullity in that I can perceive it; and since it is anchored in its physical support, it is also public. The image, therefore, is a strange hybrid – a *perceptual fiction*. That status, however, makes possible what I call the image's "hospitality". Because it is nothing itself, it can accommodate in the mode of imagery anything capable of being experienced – perceived and imagined things, people, and events; moods; even ideas.

Husserl says that art offers us an infinite realm of such perceptual fictions. It can do so because artists are creative and the realm of experience they embody in their images is infinite. Image-consciousness opens us up to that realm by bringing it inside the image. There we can see and contemplate it. The image, by the way, does not have to be exclusively visual. Husserl shows convincingly that a theatrical performance, for example, offers images that have subjects, whether real of imagined.

Husserl's discussion of the three objects in image-consciousness can be exploited in aesthetics in a multitude of fruitful ways, since all three play roles in aesthetic experience, which Husserl takes to be concerned with appearances and not with existence. Even the material support of the image can be vital to the way in which the image appears and is appreciated – the marble or bronze from which a sculpture is made shines through the image and becomes a significant factor in shaping how we experience the work.

Husserl claims that all works of art are images, though not all images are works of art. One might well wonder whether this claim can be justified, particularly in the case of modern non-figurative art and art-world phenomena such as Duchamp's ready-mades. Is a large, perfectly flat expanse of color punctuated by a few stripes, such as Barnett Newman's *Vir Heroicus Sublimis*, truly an image? Does it have a subject? Obviously not in the sense in which the photograph of the Flatiron Building has a subject. Still, Newman claimed that the painting was about something–roughly, the heroic and sublime nature of humanity – and that what one sees in the painting when one looks at it is about that. This suggests that Newman thought that he had created a meaningful image with a subject and had not simply decorated a piece of canvas in an interesting way.

The case of the "ready-mades" – the snow shovel Duchamp displayed in a gallery, for example –is more difficult still. One might be able to show that it too is an image, but, phenomenologically, that may be a stretch. I have argued, however, that perhaps there are other resources in Husserlian phenomenology and in recent analytic philosophy that could be brought to bear here. Specifically, I have in mind Husserl's *Crisis* with its discussion of cultural worlds nestled within or founded on the life-world. The latter offers a way of showing how a specific cultural world with its unique history and conditions – what Arthur Danto and George Dickie call the "artworld" – might provide the context in which artifacts produced, or, in the case of the ready-mades, selected, by an artist and made available to an "artworld public" (the community of artists, dealers, audiences for art, and so on) can be works of art, even if they are not images in the usual sense. (Duchamp himself once said that his ready-mades were not works of art; whatever they were, however, he did continue making them for many years, and their influence on subsequent artists has been immense.)

A final point about Husserl's account of image-consciousness. It enabled him to break free of the "image theory" as an account of the constitution of phantasy and memory. The image theory asserts that the object of phantasy or memory is an image internal to consciousness, something like a picture in a box. After all, how else could we be aware of a phantasied object that never existed or of a remembered object that no longer exists? Husserl subscribed to this theory early in his career, but once his view of image-consciousness matured, he criticized it and finally surrendered it altogether. He came to see that when we phantasy something we are aware of the phantasied object *itself*, not a picture of it in the mind. I can indeed view an image of a unicorn in a museum, but when I imagine a unicorn I see the unicorn itself in the mode of phantasy. Similarly, when I remember my mother, I remember her and not a picture of her. It is true that my mother is not there "in person," but it is nonetheless my mother herself and not some surrogate that I am remembering. To remember my mother or to phantasy a unicorn is not to look at an image. Husserl's conclusion here scandalizes even some phenomenologists, but it seems to me that he is on solid phenomenological ground. Image-consciousness is found exclusively when we are aware of an image with a physical support, such as a photograph of my mother or a tapestry of a unicorn. Of course, that still leaves us with the question of how phantasy is constituted, but that would take us beyond the scope of this interview.

3. What is the proper role of phenomenology in relation to other disciplines?

Phenomenology is philosophy. As such, it is not its business to compete with non-philosophical disciplines on their own turf. On the other hand, phenomenology can complement other disciplines, and do so in the process of achieving its own ends. The sciences, particularly the social sciences, regularly deal with phenomena that we experience every day, and yet our understanding of what they are is often vague and confused. What Augustine said of time is true of many other things as well. They have not been subjected to the sort of rigorous phenomenological reflection that might uncover their essential structures. It seems obvious that a discipline must have a clear idea of the phenomena it is trying to explain. Phenomenology can surely help in that respect.

In some cases, a substantial level of dialogue may be possible between phenomenology and science. Something on this order is occurring between phenomenology and cognitive science, which is the focus of a journal and to which some of the best scholars in the field are contributing important and interesting work. To say that phenomenology should not compete with other disciplines does not mean that it should ignore their findings when they enrich the range of possibilities available to phenomenological reflection. The injunction to return to the things themselves and avoid unexamined presuppositions is not an invitation to philosophical naivety. Indeed, it can even mean precisely to take up the results that other disciplines have provided. An adequate phenomenology of art, for example, would be impossible if it ignored the treasure trove of material that art history provides.

4. What have been the most significant advances in phenomenology?

This is a broad question that could be answered in many ways. I will make only one observation. Some Heideggerians, disciples of Merleau-Ponty, or phenomenological deconstructionists, among others, maintain that they have "gone beyond" Husserlian phenomenology in the sense that they believe that they have shown that it has fatal limitations. Such claims are usually based on one or more misconceptions of Husserl's thought – of the reduction, for example, or of the transcendental Ego or the nature of Husserl's "idealism" and "rationalism." It seems to me, however, that if Husserl's phenomenological project is properly understood, it not only can accommodate but even demand the developments that Heidegger or Merleau-Ponty represent. Their thought goes beyond Husserl, not in the sense that it replaces or surpasses his phenomenology, but in the sense that it fills it out, realizes projects that Husserl did not have the time to develop or that simply did not occur to him. I stress here that this is the case only if one gives a certain reading of Husserl, one that sees his phenomenology as capable of being expanded in ways that he had not foreseen. The spirit of Husserlian phenomenology, as I see it, is precisely one of generosity and cooperation in the service of truth. Given this understanding of Husserl, Merleau-Ponty's thought and Heidegger's earlier work, to take just two key examples from the phenomenological movement, represent profoundly important advances in fulfilling Husserl's vision of phenomenology as a universal science of phenomena. This is not to say, of course, that there are no limitations and problems associated with Husserl's thought or, for that matter, with the positions of Heidegger and Merleau-Ponty. If phenomenology is a philosophy of infinite tasks, the infinity refers not only to the fields to be explored but to the scrutiny that must be given to what has already been discovered.

5. What are the most important open problems in phenomenology and what are the prospects for progress?

I am not sure that the three problems or, perhaps better, "possibilities" for exploration that I mention here would be viewed as important by many others, but they are important to me.

There is a profound need for a reflection on the relationship, or absence of relationship, between the consciousness of time as Husserl and other phenomenologists have investigated it and the time of physical science. Given the importance of science in contemporary life and the prominence of time in modern physics, to leave this relationship unexamined seems phenomenologically irresponsible. Of course, only a mind well-versed in both phenomenology and science would be capable of undertaking this task.

Another theme and one central to Husserl's thought involves his conception of the transcendental Ego, which has been both embraced and criticized since it first appeared in Husserl's texts early in the last century. I have tried to show in sketchy form that the Ego is another name for the unity and identity of consciousness, that it is not simply a "pole" inhabiting consciousness, that it involves multiple levels of constitution, and that time-consciousness is fundamental to each of them. Conceived in this way, the Ego is a rich field demanding the sort of thorough investigation it has never received.

The phenomenology of cultural worlds and the nature of their constitution is another area in which more needs to be done. This is a rich theme, involving the life-world, communal existence, tradition, freedom and creativity, and history. A sound phenomenological aesthetics, to take just one example, requires an essential understanding of what it is to be a cultural world.

Phenomenology thrives on open questions, and it offers remarkable resources to the philosopher willing to come to grips with them. One can be confident that phenomenology will make progress, even as its tasks remain infinite.

4

David Carr

Professor Emeritus
Emory University (U.S.A.)

---

1. Why were you initially drawn to phenomenology?

As a student, sampling various disciplines, I somehow couldn't be satisfied with settling on one of them. I wanted to know everything, or at least I wanted to know what it would mean to know everything. As an incipient philosopher, I wanted to grasp the Big Picture. Each science looked at a different part of reality, so the solution to my dissatisfaction seemed clear. Wouldn't it just be a matter of adding all the sciences together? The only problem seemed to be figuring out how they all fit together, which meant figuring out how the parts of reality fit together. No small task, but it seemed doable in principle. And it gave philosophy something to do over and above the particular sciences. Philosophy would then just be the super science, the science of the whole of reality as opposed to the sciences of its parts. It just had to be sure not to leave anything out.

It was Descartes and then Kant who made me aware that this approach leaves something out in principle, and what it leaves out is what the whole picture depends on: subjectivity. It is for the subject that reality exists; it is the subject that claims to know anything about the world. The subjective turn, later called the transcendental turn, is what characterizes modern philosophy. It recognizes that ideas of reality, whether the whole or its parts, are sustained by a subjective grasp.

Of course, if subjectivity is left out of the Big Picture, why not just put it back in and make it the object of a science of its own? Isn't this what psychology does? That way we would close the gap and cover everything. But this would presuppose the very thing it was trying to understand: subjectivity—not as another object in the world, or domain of objects, but as that which makes objects possible at all, including the objects of psychology. This was approximately Kant's critique of Descartes' response to his discovery of the problem of subjectivity. The treatment of subjectivity had to be "transcendental," that is, not as an object in the world but precisely in its capacity of making objects and world possible. Transcendental subjectivity is world-sustaining or world-constituting subjectivity.

It was in phenomenology that I encountered the best attempt to go beyond Kant and take seriously this understanding of subjectivity. I first discovered this in early Heidegger, but as I later learned, those aspects of Heidegger's work that most impressed me were those he had taken over from Husserl: intentionality, temporality, worldhood. Many aspects of Heidegger's work, even his early work, seemed to derive from a larger, non-phenomenological agenda. Thus I was led back to Husserl as the core of the phenomenological approach to subjectivity.

2. What are your main contributions to the field of phenomenology?

After being dawn to phenomenology, in the manner described in the previous response, and after having studied Husserl's works intensely as a graduate student, I undertook to translate Husserl's *The Crisis of European Sciences*. Here was Husserl once again trying to lay out and justify his phenomenological approach, but what struck me as new in this text, compared to earlier attempts, was the broad historical framework in which Husserl placed his efforts. History seemed to be everywhere in this text, and in many different roles. Husserl wanted to show that phenomenology responded to the demands of the history of philosophy, and represented its culmination, for one thing. But this in turn was couched in a general theory of the historical character of consciousness and indeed of philosophy itself. In some ways Husserl seemed to be embracing the Diltheyan historicism that he had rejected in his 1910 essay "Philosophy as Rigorous Science." There phenomenology was portrayed as capable of transcending its historical circumstances. Now it seemed embedded in historicity.

This seemed to constitute an internal problem for Husserl's phenomenology, and I explored this problem, without resolving it, in my first book, *Phenomenology and the Problem of History*. But it also opened up for me the more general question of the relation between phenomenology and history. There were many questions arising under the rubric of the philosophy of history—the nature of the historical process, our knowledge and experience of the past, and role of history in our lives—that could be illuminated, it seemed to me, by a phenomenological treatment. This could be undertaken, I thought, without reference to the problem of the historical or trans-historical status of phenomenology itself. In other words, it would be a way of doing phenomenology, rather than meta-phenomenology; a way of applying phenomenology to an important sphere of human experience.

Most of the work that I have done since my first book has been devoted to developing a phenomenology of history in this sense, as a systematic application of the phenomenological method to history: that is, to historical knowledge, historical experience, historical existence. The fundamental concepts of phenomenology—intentionality, temporality, worldhood, intersubjectivity—can be seen at work in relation to history, as I have tried to show. Narrative, a key concept in history, can be illuminated by reference to these concepts, especially temporality and intersubjectivity. More recently I have tried to show that narrativity rests on an underlying and pervasive historical experience. The distinctive intentionality of this historical experience — its intersubjectivity, its temporality, its world — can illuminate our historical existence, our knowledge of the past, and our metaphysical attempts to comprehend history as a whole.

3. What is the proper role of phenomenology in relation to other disciplines?

The move to the transcendental turn and to transcendental subjectivity that I described in the first response above might seem to suggest a rather strict response to this question. The strict response, and this would be Husserl's, is that phenomenology's task is to examine the underlying and unquestioned presuppositions of the several sciences, which are the conditions of their possibility. This would include mapping the various domains they survey and the categories into which they fall: formal vs. material sciences, the latter breaking down into those of nature, of the psychic, and of the spirit. This is the logic and philosophy of science that Husserl outlined in his middle, "transcendental" period through the 1920s. A significant dimension is added in the *Crisis* texts of the 1930s: the sciences need to be traced back to the prescientific life-world. But this has never seemed to me to be a major innovation, and is hinted at in earlier work. The life-world just represents a deeper understanding of those underlying presuppositions that make the sciences possible.

What is "strict" about this response is that it carefully distinguishes any scientific results from those of a transcendental-phenomenological inquiry. The latter, while it is certainly scientific, is a totally different animal from mundane sciences, and it might be said that there is no interaction between the two. But Husserl admitted, especially in the later 1920s, that psychology occupied a special place in this scheme because its object was in some sense the same as that of phenomenology: consciousness. He imagined phenomenology having an effect on psychology by employing its basic concepts to clarify the psychological understanding of consciousness.

Could psychological research in turn be useful for transcendental phenomenology? Husserl didn't think so. It was left to Merleau-Ponty and Sartre to open up this possibility. And if psychology, why not other "human" sciences like sociology, anthropology, and history? Why not psychoanalysis, linguistics and even literature? Today, cognitive and neuroscience offer similar opportunities. To me, the enrichment of phenomenology by this means is far more important than doctrinal orthodoxy, even though I perfectly understand the motives behind the latter. But some caution is called for. These disciplines have their own doctrinal orthodoxies and metaphysical commitments, which must be strictly avoided and always remain bracketed by phenomenological inquiry. As long as phenomenology maintains its metaphysical neutrality it can profit by interaction with other disciplines without compromising itself.

4. What have been the most significant advances in phenomenology?

Husserl had developed the basic concepts and procedures of the phenomenological approach by 1913. As I've said, in my view the basic concepts are intentionality, temporality, world and intersubjectivity. The basic procedure is the transcendental turn embodied in the phenomenological reduction. The most important advances over this initial phase were accomplished jointly, in my view, by the early Heidegger and Merleau-Ponty. Both expanded and deepened the understanding of intentionality by taking it beyond the cognitive sphere. Heidegger saw that cognitive and scientific intentionality was grounded in a broader, pre-cognitive being-in-the-world (as he preferred to call it), and that objectivity presupposed a pre-objective and encompassing world horizon. In this he anticipated Husserl's development of the life-world. What was sorely neglected in his account, and what was supplied by Merleau-Ponty's early work, was the role of the lived body in our engagement with the world. Both of these developments were implicit in Husserl's work, and some argue that Husserl's understanding of the lived body was deeper than Merleau-Ponty's. But the latter deserves credit for making embodiment central to the phenomenological outlook.

These advances are important in their own right and have added to the scope and depth of phenomenological investigations. But they are also important for another reason. They make it possible to de-couple the concept on intentionality from those notions with which it was originally and usually associated, namely the mind, the ego, even consciousness. Merleau-Ponty is saying that the true subject of perceptual intentionality is not the mind but the body. To be sure, our understanding of the body must be re-figured and understood not as the objective but as the subjective body. In a similar way, for Heidegger intentionality is the broader practical field of operations he calls being-in-the-world. If intentionality can thus be found elsewhere than in the traditional concept of the subject, then maybe it can be discovered even beyond the individual. Here the idea of the first-person plural or we-subject suggests itself. It offers a phenomenological understanding of social existence that goes beyond even the phenomenological concept of intersubjectivity, which remains based in the notion of the individual subject. I have experimented with this concept in some of my own work and it is now much discussed by other phenomenologists as well.

5. What are the most important open problems in phenomenology and what are the prospects for progress?

Two open problems occur to me. In keeping with my response to question 3, I think that neuroscience, cognitive science and artificial intelligence overlap with phenomenology in rather obvious ways even though their attitudes and basic concepts are miles apart. More work needs to be done on both the overlap and the differences. Only if these basic conceptual relations are clarified can the two sides complement each other and mutually contribute to concrete work. Neuro- and cognitive science were for a long time linked to a "philosophy of mind" that amounted to a metaphysical commitment to reductionism. This greatly inhibited their fields of operations, and they gradually realized that they could go about their business without solving this "hard problem." The link between conscious experience and the brain can be fruitfully explored without trying to reduce the one to the other. Phenomenologists, in turn, have their own prejudices to overcome, and have to learn to see the brain as just another aspect of embodiment. Hidden and unacknowledged metaphysical commitments are the problem on both sides. To deal with them it is not enough to acknowledge them. Once acknowledged, they must also be neutralized. These are difficult problems, but progress is already being made.

The second open problem I would name has to do with metaphysical commitments as well, but in a different way. In the last paragraph I hinted that phenomenologists sometimes have a hidden commitment to idealism. Others may have a hidden commitment to realism. The open problem is this: what is the status of metaphysical commitment in general, whether idealist or realist, in relation to phenomenology? I believe that metaphysics is what Kant called a natural disposition of reason (*Naturanlage der Vernunft*). The philosophical discipline that goes by that name is just the literary expression of the hidden commitments we all have to the reality of the world and of our experience. Kant was right in thinking that when metaphysics tries to be a science it ends up being dialectical and illusory. But he was just as interested in why we ask metaphysical questions as in showing that they could not be answered. His transcendental turn amounted to the project of trying to understand metaphysics as a *Naturalage* rather than indulging our inclination to engage in it. But this project runs deeply against the grain of both reason and experience.

Husserl did something similar when he introduced the *epoche* in *Ideas* I. Developed into the transcendental-phenomenological reduction, it amounted to a systematic commitment to resist our metaphysical urges, the better to understand them. Husserl never lost sight of how difficult this is, sometimes calling it "artificial" and even "unnatural." The urge is so strong that in the end I think, Kant succumbed to it, thereby becoming the founder of German Idealism, that extravagant orgy of metaphysical speculation.

Did Husserl also succumb? I'm not sure. But I don't think *we* should. Instead, I think we need something like a "phenomenology of metaphysics," which attempts to understand our metaphysical urges without indulging them. Can this be done? I'm not sure. This could be called *our* "hard problem."

5

Steven Crowell

Joseph and Joanna Nazro Mullen Professor of Humanities
Department of Philosophy, Rice University (U.S.A.)

---

1. Why were you initially drawn to phenomenology?
I came to philosophy in a fairly roundabout way, and my attraction to phenomenology was pivotal in that. Prior to enrolling at the University of California Santa Cruz, in 1970, I would not have thought that philosophy was a candidate for serious academic study. As an adolescent, I did have an interest in some aspects of eastern and western religion, and I was a bit of a contrarian (which I guess counts as having an interest in argument), but my frame of mind was primarily scientific, and I didn't really see how philosophy could be pursued in that sort of collaborative spirit. At the same time, I was deeply drawn to the world of the ancient Greeks through their myths, and so I took a two-quarter course on Greek philosophy my first year at UCSC, one that also dealt with the legacy of the "ancient quarrel between philosophy and poetry." It was a really innovative and exciting course, and I loved it. In the third quarter of that year I tried a further course in philosophy, this one covering the modern period, and while I liked Descartes very much, it would be many years before I could take Leibniz and Spinoza, let alone Locke or Hume, seriously. The teacher of the Greek course was Paul Lee, a student of Paul Tillich and a former associate of Timothy Leary, and the following year he taught a graduate seminar on Kierkegaard which, for some reason, I was allowed to attend. We read all of the translated works, and Kierkegaard just blew me away. In part it was his Socratism, and in part it was the intricacy and beauty of his writing. But mostly it was his relentless pursuit of subjectivity. All the things that irritated me about Leibniz and Spinoza were well diagnosed by Kierkegaard (I was then totally innocent of Hegel): the idea that one could grasp subjectivity by means of "objective" thought seemed to me at least paradoxical and perhaps wholly absurd. What one could grasp that way was not, it seemed to me, what mattered about subjectivity. Later, I would understand this to be the difference between the properties of things and the meaning of things, but that was a long way off.

What does all this have to do with phenomenology? Well, I began to wonder what sort of field academic philosophy actually was and resolved to explore it further. Fortuitously, the next quarter Maurice Natanson taught a course called Recent European Philosophy which was devoted to Husserl ("Philosophy as Rigorous Science" and *Ideas I*), with some Sartre and others thrown in. I have to say that I understood almost nothing of what we read, but I did realize that Natanson was talking about exactly the issues that I'd been struggling with in the Kierkegaard seminar – how subjectivity eluded scientific psychology, for example, or what it might mean to say that "subjectivity is the truth." But he seemed to be doing so in the name of a philosophical *science* of subjectivity: phenomenology! At bottom, I think it was Husserl's emphasis on ultimate epistemic self-responsibility in philosophy – his concept of *Evidenz* and the radically first-personal project entailed by this "ethics" – that intrigued me, though I could not have named it at the time. In any case, over the Christmas recess I decided to work through *Ideas I* line by line, to see if I could figure out how it was supposed to hang together – the reductions, "pure" consciousness, intentionality, and the rest. I've never really stopped doing that, and I hope I have made some progress.

Natanson taught courses on existentialism, philosophy in literature, philosophy of the social sciences, philosophy of history, and others, all of which were grounded in his brand of phenomenology and all of which I took. Phenomenology was now pretty much *all* of philosophy for me. The scope and flexibility of its descriptive approach allowed for "application" in many of my other studies, and it began to seem that one could devote one's life to it. An "infinite task"! In contrast, I did not particularly care for what I knew of the analytic tradition at that time. If philosophy was a science, as phenomenology suggested, it had to be more that the "handmaid to the sciences" that appeared to be its lot in my analytic courses. Hadn't Kierkegaard disposed of that notion long ago? So I took courses that moved in another direction, toward the arts and poetry, many of them taught by Albert Hofstadter. There was a phenomenological connection there too, through Heidegger, but one mediated by Kant and German Idealism. I didn't want to have to choose between those two paths, and I still don't. My way of negotiating the undeniable differences between Husserlian and Heideggerian approaches to philosophy, then, and the sedimentations of tradition that they differently embody, has been to develop an independent conception of what is essential to phenomenology that can serve as a criterion for assessing their work. In struggling for decades to understand Husserl and Heidegger my conviction has been that while their writings pursue many diverse agendas, only some of these are of specifically phenomenological interest. If one is primarily interested in phenomenological philosophy, then, as I am, one is free – and perhaps obliged – to pursue those matters that stand up to phenomenological scrutiny while rejecting or ignoring the rest. That's as close as one is going to get, I think, to a communal project or science in philosophy. A phenomenologist should never be an "Husserlian" or a "Heideggerian," or whatever. Phenomenology is not a school but a way of doing philosophy.

2. What are your main contributions to the field of phenomenology?

That, of course, is for others to decide, but the question puts me in a curious position. For it may well be that what I think of as my main contribution to phenomenology is, for others, just what disqualifies me from the field altogether – namely, my tendency to think that what is distinctive of phenomenological inquiry is its focus on normatively informed meaning. This is what defines (or ought to define) the phenomenological approach to consciousness, being, phenomenality, and other such concepts. For some, my interest in normativity veers away from what is distinctly phenomenological toward the more mainstream concerns of analytic philosophy. Phenomenologists tend to understand such concerns in much the way Husserl understood Paul Natorp's neo-Kantianism – namely, as motivated from the "top down" by logical construction, conceptual presuppositions, and dialectical argumentation, rather than from the "bottom up" by descriptions of how such constructions are evidentially grounded in pre-reflective consciousness, the proto-logic of perceptual experience, and the sedimentations of the absolute temporal flow. But while I do think that this "proto" dimension can be explored phenomenologically to a certain extent, the main *philosophical* reason for doing so, I think, is to better understand intentional – that is, meaningful – experience. I don't claim that locating phenomenology in the "space of meaning" is at all original with me; on the contrary, my claim is that this is what Husserl had in view in the distinctive concept of consciousness (with its "thoroughly peculiar 'forms'") that emerged in his theory of the transcendental reduction. Similarly, I argue that whatever Heidegger meant by "being," the phenomenologically defensible takeaway is the distinction between an entity and what it is/means to be that entity. But today, many Husserlians seem to think that a position is phenomenologically significant only if it "genetically" pursues intentional content back to modes of consciousness that lack normative structure, and many Heideggerians seem to believe that the latter's real phenomenological contribution consists in his break with transcendental "subjectivism" in favor of an ontology of the "event," or "life," or "history." I remain unconvinced. As I see it, such proposals are to be judged on the basis of whether they are necessary for an account of normatively grounded meaning (i.e., canonical intentionality). *That* is our best point of reference for assessing their possible validity, and in the absence of such a point of reference we are left to accept or reject them, according to our whim, as more or less interesting speculative visions.

This insistence on there being some check on the validity of philosophical claims (some *nachvollziehbar* way of establishing how such claims could be *seen* to succeed or fail) is how I understand the phenomenological principle of *Evidenz* and the corresponding notion of philosophical self-responsibility. This motivates my argument that phenomenological philosophy is essentially a form of transcendental philosophy. More broadly, to retain its distinctive epistemic authority (which is *not* an "apodictic foundation" as this is usually conceived), phenomenology cannot abandon its focus on intentional correlation in favor of who-knows-what new form of metaphysics or dialectics. In earlier work I phrased this defense of the transcendental character of phenomenology as the difference between "straightforward" and "reflective" inquiry. Phenomenological philosophy is what one gets when one adopts the reflective stance and remains exclusively within it, and doing so already enacts the reduction in its own self-understanding. I still think that reflection picks out the key *topos* of philosophical inquiry – namely, *experience* as a descriptively accessible correlation-structure – but now I think that it is equally important to emphasize that the meaning which belongs essentially to this experience is normatively structured. For instance, experiencing something *as* a snake, tree, or apple has conditions of satisfaction that are right there *in* the experience, at stake in it, and the "operation" of such normative conditions must therefore be *described;* neither producing a logical reconstruction nor postulating neurological or cognitive "representations" can do the job. If this is true, then whatever ground is attained by a phenomenological reflection on conditions of possibility – or, put otherwise, whatever is supposed to account for the constitution of meaning – must be something that is responsive to norms *as normative*. This puts strong constraints on what can be invoked in phenomenological explanations – that is, in descriptions (and their eidetic transformations) of what purports to be necessary and jointly sufficient for intentional content.

3. What is the proper role of phenomenology in relation to other disciplines?

If phenomenology is understood as careful attention to the way things show up for us in first-person experience, then it can play a variety of roles in relation to other disciplines. No one could deny that phenomenology has made important contributions to (and has, in turn, derived valuable impetus from) fields as diverse as psychopathology, sociology, literary theory, cognitive science, medicine, environmental studies, gender studies, and many others. I don't think that one will find another philosophical approach that has been even remotely as productive in fostering interdisciplinary work. Sometimes that contribution is in a critical vein. For instance, phenomenological reflection can identify points at which physicalist presuppositions distort the way questions about perceptual content are raised in cognitive psychology. As Husserl said already in relation to the psychology of his time: those who deny the importance of "armchair" descriptions of first-person experience in the study of perception, insisting on nothing but what can be confirmed experimentally, must already appeal to such experience to determine whether their experiments actually have perception in view at all. Sometimes the contribution is more positive. For instance, phenomenological reflections on embodiment and temporality have contributed directly to work in cognitive science, and phenomenological approaches to intersubjectivity have important implications for those social sciences that do not pursue an exclusively quantitative agenda. But if we are talking about phenomenological *philosophy*, then the relation looks different – at least to me.

Philosophy is a distinctive sort of inquiry with its own norms and stakes, and those stakes must be pursued largely from within what Husserl called the "reduction." That is, philosophy can borrow nothing from the other sciences as premises for its own inquiry. There are complicated reasons for this commitment to the autnomony of philosophy *vis-à-vis* empirical and formal sciences, but Husserl was quite right to insist on it, as was Heidegger. Husserl introduced these considerations in his critique of "naturalism," but what he really had in mind is what we would now call "scientism." There need be no necessary conflict between "consciousness" and "nature" in all possible understandings of these terms. Rather, what Husserl objected to (as did Heidegger) was the idea that natural science should be allowed to dictate the terms in which philosophical questions are asked and answered. This is not at all to be anti-*science*, and it allows plenty of room for a phenomenological "naturalism" as pursued by Merleau-Ponty, for example, or even for a "phenomenology naturalized," so long as the latter does not collapse the distinction between entities and the meaning thanks to which those entities can be identified and become objects of knowledge for us.

This does, however, raise the question of how to understand the exchange or symbiosis between phenomenological philosophy and empirical scientific work. To my mind, the relation is far from clear today, and this is especially dangerous when the importance of any kind of intellectual work is increasingly measured by how much "real science" it contains. The empirical sciences do not speak with a single voice; hence the phenomenologist will have to determine *which* findings and *which* theories and *which* sciences are to be taken as philosophical touchstones. Given that the phenomenologist is usually not an actual practitioner of these sciences, the answer to such questions will not come easily. As things now stand, the answer all too frequently is: whatever findings, theories, and sciences confirm one's prior philosophical commitments.

Finally, phenomenological reflection can reveal the normative commitments of sciences as they are currently practiced, and someday this might be of interest to those sciences – though now it is of interest only to the *philosophy* of science as practiced in a phenomenological way.

4. What have been the most significant advances in phenomenology?

The ongoing publication of the *Husserliana* series and of Heidegger's *Gesamtausgabe* has given us an insight into their work unavailable to previous generations, and this has, not surprisingly, yielded a deeper sense both for the nature of phenomenology itself and for its contributions to philosophy. I won't comment in this context on specific advances in the interpretation of Husserl, Heidegger, and other phenomenologists, but if we focus on advances in philosophy that phenomenological work has occasioned, a number of examples come to mind. For instance, phenomenology has provided a set of tools that allow us to think about intentional content in ways that avoid problems arising from standard "representationalist" approaches to the mind. This is connected with phenomenological work that emphasizes both the mind's embodiment and the practical context of conscious experience in ways that elude more mainstream, generally third-person, approaches. This, in turn, has opened up a conception of the relation between mind and world that breaks with the still-standard Cartesian assumptions in debates over "content." The phenomenological approach is increasingly recognized as operating on the far side of dichotomies such as internalism/externalism or immanent/transcendent. This has been facilitated by phenomenological analyses that demonstrate how deeply intersubjectivity cuts in any account of intentionality. Phenomenology has much to contribute to what is increasingly recognized as an ineliminable "second-person" dimension to all experience.

Related to this, some of the most significant advances in recent phenomenology are found in the area of ethics. This was not much of an issue for the first generations of phenomenologists, but the "post-positivist" turn in analytic philosophy has brought with it a new interest in normative ethics and value-theory, which provides a context for appreciating phenomenological contributions in this area. For instance, descriptions of the "founding" relations between cognitive, evaluative, and practical intentionalities (building upon work by Husserl, Scheler, and Levinas, among others) provide a more nuanced access to problems such as acting for reasons or moral motivation than does mainstream "belief/desire" moral psychology. In turn, the recent interest among mainstream ethicists in finding ways to bridge the gap between value-theoretical and deontological approaches has contributed to a better understanding of what is at stake in, and entailed by, the reflections of the canonical phenomenologists.

Beyond philosophy of mind and moral psychology, there is a good deal of work being done today in what might be called the phenomenology of the formal sciences (logic, mathematics, mereology), and equally in the interpretive fields of history, literary theory, anthropology, and religion. As is the case in philosophy of mind and moral psychology, the best of this work does not treat phenomenology as a one-way street: it engages with other philosophical approaches and encounters in them both implicit tendencies toward phenomenological insights and also biases that in turn can be overcome by making these phenomenological tendencies explicit and developing them more fully.

5. What are the most important open problems in phenomenology and what are the prospects for progress?

Since I think of phenomenology as a way of doing philosophy rather than as a system or research program that has open problems, I must approach this question indirectly. On the one hand, the open problems of phenomenology would simply be the open problems of philosophy, and those, in a certain sense, *stay* open since there is always more to be said about whatever stage has been reached in a given discussion. Right now, phenomenologists seem to be well engaged in philosophical discussions concerning, among other things, how to integrate the first-person exploration of consciousness and intentionality into various scientific approaches to nature; how perception can serve a justificatory role in knowledge; how to think about self-identity; and how to understand the experiences that ground our social world. Beyond that, one obvious question that has consumed a lot of attention lately concerns the so-called "theological turn" in phenomenology. Despite all the heat, I think that the whole idea of a "phenomenology of religious experience" is as yet not very well understood.

This, it seems to me, is actually a sub-heading of an even larger set of issues on the horizon – namely, how we are to understand the relation between phenomenology, as a way of doing philosophy, and "metaphysics." Again, there has been a lot of recent work on this topic, but some very fundamental issues seem to be sidestepped in much of the literature. Both Husserl and Heidegger, for instance, saw phenomenology as a way of investigating the disclosure of that meaning through which entities can be given, rather than as a direct investigation into properties of entities. In contrast, it is commonly thought that metaphysics investigates properties, causes, and principles of entities. So the question arises: by what means does phenomenology segue from a transcendental or ontological concern with meaning to a determination of entities as such – what Husserl called "ultimate facta" and Heidegger called "metontology"? It has always seemed to me that the positive sciences explore the properties of entities and that Kant was right to think that philosophy ("pure reason") has no special access to "more basic" properties hidden from those sciences. Hence metaphysics, in this sense, is not a cognitively grounded inquiry. When it seeks to establish a cognitive ground by drawing premises from the positive sciences, it becomes a certain kind of world-view. Some phenomenological "metaphysics" is pursued in a similar way: a certain concept that derives from phenomenological reflection on first-person experience (e.g., desire, possibility, normative claim) is inflated into a fundamental principle of the whole of what is. But do such phenomenologically developed concepts retain their meaning and authority when extended to domains where no first-person evidence is possible? That's an open question.

Of course, there are other conceptions of what metaphysics amounts to. A currently very popular one in analytic philosophy proceeds in terms of possible worlds without any reference to phenomenological considerations, and this is formally mirrored, on the continental side, by speculative realism and its kin. Such approaches also pose challenges to the claims – in comparison, very modest ones – of transcendental phenomenology. How, most generally, should phenomenology respond to the "new rationalism" in metaphysics, to purely formal and mathematical approaches to the fundamental questions of philosophy?

Yet the most pressing open problem for phenomenology arrives from an altogether different direction: how is the practice of phenomenology to be communicated to future generations in ways that foster independent philosophical thinking? The situation may be different elsewhere, but in the United States the prospects for an efflorescence of phenomenology seem dim, despite the fact that increasingly there is a substantive convergence between phenomenological and mainstream philosophical concerns. The problem is that it is very difficult for students to develop a facile and disciplined practice of phenomenological reflection. The usual approach is to lose oneself in the books of its founders, but this yields two deeply linked problems. First, the writings of all the major phenomenologists tend to be both wide-ranging and hermetic, so that an overview of even their major themes and contributions is very difficult to attain. Add to this the fact that in the case of Husserl, much of his most important phenomenological work is found scattered in his vast and only sporadically translated *Nachlass*, and you have the makings of a second problem: this method of becoming a phenomenologist has produced some extremely keen and perceptive scholarship, but given the current structure of academic study, it may not leave the student much time for developing an independent philosophical perspective. This makes it difficult for those who proceed in this way to engage with philosophers of other persuasions, since everything must first be translated back into the language of Husserl or Heidegger or Merleau-Ponty. I myself certainly admit to being guilty of this failing, but I am convinved that another way must be found to transmit the phenomenological heritage.

Taking Husserl as an example, perhaps we need to edit and translate collections devoted to specific philosophical topics, drawing excerpts from different volumes of the *Husserliana*. This could highlight Husserl's own practice – rather than his meta-reflections on that practice – and provide examples of how to address issues in ethics, action theory, or epistemology in a phenomenological way without first having to decide debates about the reduction, the transcendental ego, and all the rest. Similar volumes could be drawn from the writings of classical and contemporary phenomenologists who represent different philosophical positions on a particular topic. By being focused on a substantive issue, the evident convergences and divergences might become, for the student, more than the usual invitation to profess allegiance to a name. Volumes of this sort already exist, of course, but they are not usually composed with this specifically pedagogical goal in mind.

In any case, we must find ways of presenting phenomenology as a practice that can be learned without spending years in the archives. In this respect, our situation is rather the mirror-image of the one in which analytic philosophy finds itself today. Whereas analytic philosophy developed as a set of (loosely defined and perhaps not very well understood) practices inculcated through a tradition of canonical examples rather than "founding texts" – indeed only recently have books and courses devoted to the history of analytic philosophy become fairly common – phenomenology was disseminated mainly by means of commentaries on its founders (hobbled by the political disputes that attended its founding moments) and has never developed a practical tradition in which phenomenologists respond to one another's work on philosophical problems *apart* from reference to, and commentary on, authoritative texts. There are understandable reasons for this, but to the extent that phenomenology is indeed a way of doing philosophy its future may depend on "forgetting" its history for a while and just tackling philosophical problems in a phenomenological way.

While this is certainly a daunting task, there is actually no shortage of examples of such work to draw from. This is not the place to offer shout-outs to my favorite contemporary phenomenologists, but it isn't hard to identify those who are moving phenomenological philosophy forward in a creative and original way. Students should seek them out. One characteristic that distinguishes them, in my view, is their attunement to, and engagement with, the moments of phenomenological reflection that increasingly show up (usually, but not always, without being identified as such) in the work of philosophers who do not self-describe as phenomenologists. Students intent on learning the craft of phenomenological thinking would do well to study these other philosophers too, since they too are enriching the phenomenological tradition.

6
Françoise Dastur

Honorary Professor of Philosophy

Taught philosophy in the Universities of Paris I, Paris 12 and Nice-Sophia Antipolis

---

1. Why were you initially drawn to phenomenology?

In France the study of philosophy is a must in the last year of high school. Monique Dixsaut who became later the best Plato's specialist in France was my philosophy teacher in Lyon when I did my last year of high school. I was initiated by her to Bergson, Plato and Nietzsche, the three philosophers she considered as the most important ones. One year later, when I decided to go to Paris in order to study philosophy, Merleau-Ponty had just died, and this brought me to read during the summer his *Phenomenology of Perception*. But previous to that, I had already read big portions of Sartre's *Being and Nothingness* and also Henry Corbin's translation of *What is Metaphysics*? and some other Heidegger's texts. I was therefore prepared for two encounters that have decided my philosophical orientation: Paul Ricoeur, who was then a professor at the Sorbonne, and Jacques Derrida, who taught there as an assistant and who published in 1962 his Introduction to Husserl's short and famous text on *The Origin of Geometry*. It was under their respective direction that I began the reading of Husserl's and Heidegger's works. I was then part of an informal group of students who worked on Husserl under Derrida's guidance and this was how I became involved in a very intensive study of phenomenological major texts. But many of them were not yet translated into French at that time, and I encountered so many difficulties in trying to read Heidegger's *Sein und Zeit* which was not yet translated into French, that I decided to go to Germany in order to improve my knowledge of the German language and to continue my studies there. Thanks to a scholarship from the German government, I was able to spend a year studying at the University of Freiburg-im-Breisgau, where Husserl, then Heidegger (who succeeded him) had taught. I studied there under the direction of Werner Marx, the author of *Heidegger and the Tradition*, who had just left the New School of New York in order to take up the vacant chair previously occupied by Husserl and Heidegger and I also followed the seminars of Eugen Fink, Husserl's last assistant, whose teaching was a real incitation to dedicate my researches to come to phenomenology. When I came back to France, I completed my master thesis which was dealing with Heidegger's conception of language and after that I had the good fortune of being appointed as an assistant at the Sorbonne, where, thanks to the presence of Jean-Toussaint Desanti, an eminent specialist of the philosophy of mathematics and logic and a commentator of Husserl, who was professor there I was able to devote the majority of my teaching to Husserl's works during the years that followed. If I now try to explain why I was drawn to phenomenology, I have to mention first my early interest in German philosophers and poets, such as Nietzsche and Hölderlin, which I had read in the last year of high school, and then the fact that in France phenomenology was still at the beginning of the 1960s a very "popular" kind of philosophy, Merleau-Ponty and Sartre being still considered at that time the most important French philosophers.

2. What are your main contributions to the field of phenomenology?

I think that my main contribution to phenomenology was the fact that I dedicated most of my teaching to it during the 1970s, which was the time when structuralism was the dominant philosophical current in France. I was myself teaching in the University of Paris I, the old Sorbonne having been divided into several universities after 1968, and I was there almost the only one to still believe that phenomenology had remained alive in France, at a time when the most important thinkers were Foucault, Althusser and Levi-Strauss and when Sartre was banned from the universities and Merleau-Ponty completely forgotten. Ricoeur was no longer teaching in the centre of Paris, but in the suburb, in a new university built in Nanterre, and after 1968, he began teaching many months every year in Chicago. And Derrida, who had dedicated his first works to Husserl, broke with phenomenology after the publication in 1967 of *La Grammotologie* and became as the thinker of "deconstruction" more famous in the US than in France itself. Besides my teaching on Husserl as an assistant to Desanti, I did my best in order to initiate the students to Merleau-Ponty's philosophy and to Heidegger's thinking, and I must say that I was the only one to do so in the University of Paris I until the beginning of the 1980s, when the structuralist wave receded and the revival of phenomenology began.

During all these years I dedicated myself solely to teaching and started to publish books only at the beginning of the 1990s. The first book I wrote was an introduction to Heidegger's conception of time and it was followed a few years later by another one on Husserl's philosophy considered as whole from his earlier works on mathematics and logic to the last one on history. These two small introductions to Heidegger's and Husserl's philosophy had been written mainly for students, as was also another collection of essays dealing with some important phenomenological thinkers such as Levinas, Merleau-Ponty, Patocka, and Ricoeur. I also published a collection of texts on Merleau-Ponty's at a time when his early as well as his late philosophy was rediscovered in France. Later I concentrated my work on Heidegger and published three books dealing with the topic of language and logic in Heidegger's thought, with his relation to anthropology and with his late thinking. But I also dedicated some essays and two books to the question of death and finitude which is in my view a central phenomenological question.

I also contributed to phenomenology as a translator into French of texts from Husserl, Fink, Binswanger, Boss and Szilasi, and also by being in 1993 one of the founders of the *Ecole Française de Daseinsanalyse* and by working with psychiatrists, psychologists and other philosophers in the frame of the monthly seminar I have directed since then at the Sorbonne. This was my contribution to the revival of phenomenological psychiatry which had almost completely disappeared in France after the sixties, when psychoanalysis became with Lacan the overwhelming interpretative tool of psychopathological disorders.

I consider therefore myself mainly as a teacher and in this regard, I am critical of the allusive and rhetorical way of writing and using words and concepts which has characterised French attitude concerning philosophical writing since the 1960's. I am convinced that it is possible for example to translate Heidegger in a comprehensible way. In my books on him I have used his vocabulary but in insisting on the *experience* itself that he described in such a way and not on the words as such that he used. I think that all philosophers should be read in that way, by putting the emphasis not on the verbal expression, but on the experience that these words are expressing. Merleau-Ponty is a good example of a philosopher who was also a good writer, his texts are very literary but nevertheless clear, since he is not using any kind of jargon. This was not exactly the case already with Sartre, but it became worse with Levinas and Derrida, who are sometimes quite difficult to understand, as are also Foucault and Deleuze. Clarity in the philosophical field is also an ethical issue. If you come before an audience and you are not ready to speak to them and to address them in a way that doesn't presuppose any special knowledge and use of words, then you are not doing your task as a philosopher and even less as a phenomenologist, since phenomenology means the "elucidation" of phenomena and not a mere play with words. In one of my last books which is dealing with Derrida's reading of Husserl and Heidegger, I have undertaken to show that the deconstruction of metaphysics can be achieved with phenomenology itself and not necessarily in the way Derrida understands the word "deconstruction" he himself found first in Heidegger.

3. What is the proper role of phenomenology in relation to other disciplines?

Phenomenology is not for me a theory or a discipline amongst other ones in the philosophical field, but it is, as both Husserl and Heidegger said, a concept of method, and as such it is nothing else than "the" philosophical method of addressing problems. As Husserl defined it, it is the method of going to the "things themselves" rather than remaining on the level of mere words and thus trying to have a relation with what is without having any other presuppositions than the ones which are rooted in the things themselves, as Heidegger and Gadamer said. The question is therefore not for me to defend phenomenology against other philosophical "currents", since as Merleau-Ponty himself said, in his foreword to *Phenomenology of Perception,* phenomenology exists as a movement, and not as a philosophical "school", and has to be practiced as a style or a manner of doing philosophy. The question is therefore not to immerge myself in an endless exegesis of Husserl's manuscripts or of Heidegger's complete works, since phenomenology does not consist only in reading texts but also in trying to *apply* the phenomenological method to other areas of human experience.

This is for example what I tried to show in a small book on "Heidegger and the anthropological question", since the conception of the human being as *Dasein* can become in my view the basis of a new kind of anthropology, a phenomenological anthropology, which remains to be constituted. The elaboration of such a phenomenological anthropology is the final goal of our association, the *Ecole française de Daseinsanalyse*, a research unit which is affiliated to the Husserl Archive of Paris. Other affiliated groups are working in Marseille and Nice and in the College International of Philosophy in Paris. The psychiatrists who are working with us are still a small minority, but the interest for existential analysis is slowly growing not only in France, but in other European countries, such as Schwitzerland, Italy and Belgium, and in South and North America. In our monthly seminar in the Sorbonne, we try to find a balance between the theoretical study of the literature on existential analysis, i.e. the reading of the works of the most famous representatives of Daseinsanalysis, like Binswanger and Boss on one side, and on the other side the exposition by the psychiatrists of their work with their own patients, which gives us the occasion of "applying" the phenomenological method to human behaviors.

Such a phenomenological anthropology could therefore be a new paradigm for psychiatry, since it gives a new basis for understanding the so called "mentally" ill person in which we have to see first an "existing" being and not only a medical "case". The main problem is here the therapeutic relation in which the psychiatrist has to try to understand the concrete and personal situation of his patient instead of treating him or her immediately as an object of the medical science. Phenomenological psychiatry has been developed first by Binswanger, and after that by Boss, on the basis that madness is not "abnormal" but rather another way of understanding and experiencing the world, the main problem being that mad people are suffering from their otherness and need therefore the assistance of a therapist. But trying to "understand" madness rather than to "explain" it by looking for causes implies from the therapist that he becomes aware of being himself a *Dasein*. The "phenomenological" or "existential" therapist has to change not only his perception of his patient but also his perception of himself. What is required from him or her is a total conversion of the look, in the sense that the psychiatrist has first of all to behave in regard to the patient as a human being and not as a professional. The therapeutic relation does not consist on the part of the therapist to substitute himself to the patient in order to bring him again to "normality", but to allow him as much as possible to take charge of himself and of his or her existential problem, which has to be considered not as an "objective" deficiency, but as another manner of being in the world. This does not mean however that the behavior of mad people could be completely understood in this way. But what remains enigmatic in them can be considered as similar to what remains enigmatic also for us in our own experience of the world.

4. What have been the most significant advances in phenomenology?

We usually speak of advances in the scientific domain, but phenomenology is not a science, so that it is very difficult to answer this question. If we consider the work of the founders of phenomenology, Husserl and Heidegger, we have to recognize that both of them have been able to "elucidate" quite a lot of phenomena, starting with mathematical and logical phenomena up to social and historical ones.

The most important advance was in my view the fact that both of them were able to give us a new understanding of the being of man. Husserl continued to use the word "subject" to designate the human being, but he did not understand it as a substantial entity, but rather in a dynamic and temporal way. The most important advance in this respect was his conception of temporality which allowed him to show that the constitutive activity of the subject is based on a temporal and anonymous flow for which, as he said in 1905, "names are missing". This brought him to the very important idea of the "passive synthesis", which implies that the subject is not the origin of all what happens in him. This emphasis put on the original "passivity" or "receptivity" of the subject was developed by Heidegger who refused to use the word of "subject" and gave in this way a founding role to the "affective" tonalities in the human subject, in opposition to the modern philosophical tradition which considers "affects" as epiphenomena and grants the leading role to the intellect in the constitution of experience. One important member of French phenomenology, Michel Henry, has developed further the thematic of a fundamental passivity which is the basis of his "phenomenology of life".

Another very important advance was the emphasis put on the relation to the other human being, again both by Husserl, who showed in his 5th Cartesian Meditation that real subjectivity as to be understood as a transcendental intersubjectivity, and by Heidegger who defined *Dasein* as being intrinsically *Mitsein*, being with others. The importance of the relation with the other human being was further developed in Sartre's as well as in Merleau-Ponty's writings and it took a fundamental meaning in Levinas' thinking, which I myself consider as being at the limits of phenomenology, since for him the "absolute Other", as he says, has no longer the meaning of a phenomenon.

On the other hand Merleau-Ponty's work constitutes in its entirety a very important advance of the phenomenology of corporeality, a thematic already present in Husserl, but which was developed by Merleau-Ponty in a full way, so that the bodily phenomena, which had been underestimated in classical philosophy, appeared as the fundamental element of the human phenomenon. And last but not least, both Husserl and Heidegger were able to transform in a complete manner the conception of logic and language that prevailed since Aristotle in classical philosophy : Husserl on one hand made clear that linguistic incarnation is the necessary condition of logical truth itself and Heidegger on the other hand showed that language is not a human invention but the original "event" of the clearing by which we are present to the world.

5. What are the most important open problems in phenomenology and what are the prospects for progress?

Is there something like progress in philosophy ? I doubt it. Progress is again only to be found in science whose task is to give an always more plausible explanation of what is. Philosophy, i.e. phenomenology does not aim at explaining *(erklären)* anything, but want merely to elucidate *(aufklären)* the meaning of phenomena. Therefore what can only be said is that there are still phenomena to be elucidated further. I myself tried to develop a phenomenological conception of finitude in following the hints found both in Husserl's transcendental phenomenology and in Heidegger's thinking of the event of being. This is in my view on this point that it can be shown that phenomenology is the deconstruction of traditional metaphysics since finitude has been determined in traditional philosophy in an *external* manner, i.e. as constituting a human feature in opposition to the divine conceived as infinite and absolute, so that it was considered as something *negative*. But in the phenomenological perspective, in which being and appearing are no longer opposed, a *positive* concept of finitude comes to light in relation to a new conception of time and history. This is what happens in Husserl's last philosophy where time is conferred a new ontological importance so that by rejecting the classical idea of a positive infinity, Husserl is led to develop a paradoxical conception of the "history of truth" which does not however imply relativism, but has to be understood on the basis of the intrinsic historicity of reason. And Heidegger's conception of finitude breaks even more decisively with its metaphysical conception, since Heidegger shows not only that human finitude, which is linked to the being toward death of *Dasein,* is the "concealed ground of the historicity of Dasein", but also that the meaning of being depends upon its relation to time and history. This implies that the history of the human being has to be understood on the basis of a paradoxical "history of being" which involves the intrinsic finitude of being itself.

Another problem that remains open in the phenomenological movement and which is linked to the thematic of finitude is the eurocentrism of most of its representatives, especially those who have developed a philosophy of history, like Patocka or Hannah Arendt. Only Levinas' work has shown that phenomenology can find its inspiration not only in the Greek beginning, but also elsewhere, in the Jewish tradition. Today, in this time of "globalization", we should be more open to the non European traditions than Husserl and Heidegger, who were looking mainly in the direction of the Greeks in spite of the fact that both of them had through some of their students, especially those coming from Japan, a relation to the Orient. Husserl had some contact with Buddhism and in 1925 he even published a recension of the German translation of the *Sutta Pitaka*, the teachings of Buddha, but he always maintained that Socrates remained superior to Buddha in so far as he is not led by a practical but only by a theoretical motivation. And we know that the young Heidegger was interested in Chinese philosophy and wanted to translate Laotse, and that later he entered in a dialogue with the representatives of the Kyoto school of Japan. The dialogue between phenomenology, Buddhism, and Japanese philosophy should be in my view further developed as some philosophers in the US, in Europe and in Japan, have already began to do. I am myself working at the moment on Indian Buddhism and Indian thinking in general and would like to show that the phenomenological perspective can be expanded not only through a dialogue with the Anglo-Saxon analytical philosophy or with the rapidly developing neurosciences, but also through an intercultural dialogue with the Indian tradition of thinking, in which we find not only a theory of a "transcendental" subject, the *atman*, to be compared with the Husserlian "pure ego", but also two schools of logic, the Nyaya and Vaisheshuika schools to be brought in relation with the Husserlian understanding of logic. And Heidegger's conception of language could also be put in relation with the work of Panini (4th century before the Christian era) whose theory of grammar and language was more advanced than the Western linguistic theory of the 19th and 20th century and whose work influenced modern linguists such as Bopp, Saussure, Jakobson and Chomsky.

As a conclusion I would say that in my view, phenomenology should not remain, as it is nowadays too often the case, a scholar study, since, as a concept of method, it can and should open itself not only to other areas of knowledge, to social sciences, psychiatry and anthropology, but also to the works of thought of other civilizations, particularly to eastern philosophy.

7
Nicolas de Warren

Professor of Philosophy

Husserl Archives, Center for Phenomenology and Continental Philosophy, KU Leuven (Belgium)

---

1. Why were you initially drawn to phenomenology?

I was initially drawn into phenomenology through the compelling examples of two teachers, against the backdrop of a growing realization that I could no longer become what I had first aspired to be. I began my undergraduate studies in physics with the ambition of studying quantum physics. Ever since I was young, I wanted to understand how the universe was created and what purpose, if any, there might be to human existence. In my junior year, I started to discover painfully the limitations of my mathematical capacities and my fledgling ability to generate what Richard Feynman called "physical intuitions"—a sine qua non for any future in theoretical physics. In the midst of this crisis, I enrolled from sheer curiosity in a course in the philosophy of physics taught by Abner Shimony. This course opened my eyes to philosophy, and after an advanced course in the philosophy of physics and a somewhat successful paper on Bell's Theorem, I decided to switch my major to philosophy. After having been taken by Bergson's "Introduction to Metaphysics," Shimony suggested that I take a course in phenomenology with the Czech philosopher Erazim Kohák, who in turn recommended that I continue my incipient philosophical adventure with the Polish thinker Krysztof Michalski—both of whom, along with Shimony, were teaching at Boston University.

We naturally tend to mythologize our beginnings and no less so with the origin of our personal decision to study philosophy. In hindsight, it is difficult for me to understand what it was about this first exposure to Husserl, Heidegger, and Patočka, but also, through Michalski, to Hegel and Nietzsche, that drew me into phenomenology, and thereby to philosophy. The seriousness of the devotion to think philosophically exemplified in the very different personalities of Kohák and Michalski must surely have played a significant role. When each spoke about phenomenology, I felt thrust into the presence of something tangible and alive, as if in that instant, nothing else mattered except the challenge to think philosophically. I would never have been drawn into phenomenology without having been attracted to these incomparable teachers of philosophy. Each possessed that incandescent Socratic quality of philosophical eros without which philosophy arguably devolves into mere cleverness or the shallow pride of professionalism.

This anecdotal narrative of how I came to phenomenology reveals to my mind two essential traits of phenomenological thought. In a sense not well appreciated today with the ever-spiraling professionalization of philosophy, the intellectual draw of phenomenology has always been connected to the pedagogical radiance of un maître à penser. Beginning with Husserl, but, in fact, already with Brentano, the history of the phenomenological movement, in its various twists and turns, in its heresies and orthodoxies, is essentially a history of great teachers, who, each in their own inimitable style, extended philosophy's lease on life by instilling a renewed desire for genuine philosophical creativity. It was therefore not any particular idea (intentionality, the lived-body, etc.) or particular figure (Husserl, Heidegger, etc.) that drew me into phenomenology. It was rather an odd couple of exiles — is philosophy not a perpetual form of exile? — who were responsible for my entry into phenomenology.

The draw of phenomenology is inseparable from its ambition to realize an idea of philosophy. It is less phenomenology per se, but the way in which a certain uncompromising idea of philosophy, whether as "rigorous science," "thinking of being," "wild thinking," etc., becomes set into motion that pulled me and continues to pull me into phenomenology. In taking nothing for granted of what phenomenology could be, one must take nothing for granted of what philosophy might become. Here we touch upon the fragility of phenomenological philosophy—a fragility productively exploited time and again by phenomenology itself but also, and threateningly, by the institutionalization of philosophy. This fragility—the inability of phenomenological philosophy to state definitively what it is and what it is after—is as old as philosophy itself. Did not Aristophanes ridicule Socrates in The Clouds with his biting parody of a wisdom that does not even know itself? This unknowing keeps me within phenomenology, as much as it prevents me from identifying myself entirely with it.

2. What are your main contributions to the field of phenomenology?

Recently, I have alighted upon the outlines of a more original and engaging manner in which to approach Husserl's phenomenological thinking. My proposal begins by taking seriously Husserl's claim that transcendental phenomenology is the ambition to develop a philosophical science, where the meaning of "science" as well as "philosophy" enjoy no direct historical antecedent. I understand the provocation of this proposition to consist in the effort to re-think by phenomenological means what it means to think philosophically. The main aim of this new science called transcendental phenomenology is to regenerate what it means to think philosophically and to forge a manner of thinking that, as Husserl clearly states in the Introduction to *Ideen I*, goes against our entrenched habits of thinking, including, most demandingly, the ingrained reflexes of philosophical thinking itself. This emphasis on phenomenology as responding to the question "what is called thinking?" reflects a pervasive crisis of reason that defines modernity. What calls for a renewed understanding of philosophical thought is the crisis of thinking itself. Husserl's fundamental problem, on my view, from the Logical Investigations to Crisis of the European Sciences, remained the sense and significance of reason for human existence. As Husserl trenchantly argued in the Crisis, the paradox of rationality, as paradigmatically expressed with modern natural science, is that rationality has become philosophically incomprehensible, not because it fails, but on the contrary, due to its unprecedented success. Reason remains in its own achievement unknown to itself.

The famous "principle of all principles" is the cornerstone of Husserl's phenomenology of reason. Contrary to how this "principle of all principles" has often been received, I propose to understand the centrality of intuition and evidence in Husserl's thinking as characterizing the radicality of reason. Reason names an orientation towards the world in which the sway of how the world manifests itself meets the uncompromising demand of intellectual responsibility towards the truth of the world. Evidence, for Husserl, is the principle of alterity; it characterizes the encounter with what can dispossess us of our previous knowledge, add to or detract from what we know, but also confirm what we have come to know about the world. One the great discoveries in Husserl's phenomenology of reason is the pluralization of the senses of evidence; or, in other words, different forms of manifestation are characterized by different forms of evidence: what counts as evidence in mathematics is not the same as what counts as evidence in perceptual experience. There is no uniform sense of "evidence," no meaning of Being as such. Rather than thinking the unity of Being, Husserl's phenomenology of reason attempts to think the multitude of the senses of being under the purview of the unified demand of reflection and the unwavering responsibility towards the evidence in which how the world is or is not.

The originality of Husserl's phenomenology of reason is best expressed in one of its most intractable problems. One of the defining tensions that structures Husserl's transcendental phenomenology is the one between constitution and evidence. On the one hand, objects of possible experience, as synthetic manifolds, must be constituted in transcendental consciousness, that is: objects are achievements of non-arbitrary sense-formation. Sense only has sense for consciousness, for an awareness of something having sense (or non-sense). On the other hand, given that intentionality—the fundamental structure of sense-formation, or constitution—is structured according to the dynamic between "empty" and "fulfilled" intentions, consciousness is open and directed towards how the world shows itself as itself (evidence). We thus see that, on the one hand, consciousness constitutes experience but that, on the other hand, consciousness is an openness to the world, and most significantly, directed towards an apprehension of the world in terms of evidence. Consciousness is both accountable to the world and responsible for the world.

In this manner, Husserl effectuates a reversal of Kant's Copernican Revolution with his novel conception of reason as intuition. Recall that Kant's Copernican Revolution critically depends on severing reason (*Vernunft*) from intuition (*Anschauung*): intuitions, in Kant's celebrated definition, are essentially blind, and hence the astounding paradox of Kantian intuition: it is an *Anschauung* that in itself sees nothing: to see is here essentially to be blind. The distance between *Anschauung* and *Vernunft* is measured by the intermediate faculty of understanding; understanding in synthesis with *Anschauung* produces knowledge of experience. In its spontaneous activity of recognition, understanding gives sight to blindness while *Anschauung* gives purchase (content) to recognition. Reason, on this account, does not provide any positive knowledge of the world and must thus devote itself to self-regulation; it guards against the violation of its own borders and illusions generated by its own lack of transcendental vigilance. Husserl reverses this separation—and this, I claim, is the principal accomplishment of the *Ideen I*. Rather than defining intuition as blind and reason as bereft of any positive knowledge of experience, Husserl gives insight back to intuition and defines reason as the most accomplished form of insight, or intuition. It is not the intellectual intuition devastatingly dismantled by Kant, but a discursive (i.e., synthetic) reasoning intuition that does not give form to what it sees but that sees in the form of what it is given. Truth is given back to the world much as the world is given back to philosophy.

3. What is the proper role of phenomenology in relation to other disciplines?

The question concerning the "proper" role of phenomenology towards other disciplines depends on the meaning given to "proper" as well as the type of discipline in question. Since I reject any general or generic conception of "phenomenology," one would first have to agree on the proper conception of phenomenology before venturing any pronouncement on the "proper" role of phenomenology towards other disciplines. Likewise, one would have to specify which discipline one has in mind, since, on my view, there is no one dominating "role" proper to phenomenology in relation to all other disciplines, but only different roles in view of specific disciplines. This question concerning the proper role of phenomenology is also—it is all too easily forgotten—as much an issue of the proper role of phenomenology towards itself as a claim to philosophy. How we define our roles with regard to others reflects how we define ourselves; so, too, with philosophy, and especially in the case of phenomenology, where it is unclear whether phenomenology has any exclusive propriety domain over any object (consciousness, art, mathematics, etc.). Much of the confusion and hurried assessments that characterize current thinking about the role of phenomenology towards other disciplines (for example, with regard to the experimental sciences) stems from a proper lack of reflection on the proper role of phenomenology towards itself, namely, as philosophy. Indeed, much of the vogue to apply phenomenology to X, Y, or Z mirrors unwittingly an abandonment of any robust conception of phenomenology as philosophy, or, in other words, as a commitment "to what matters most," my own preferred non-defining definition of philosophical thought, which I take freely from Plotinus.

The reason why these two considerations (what meaning to give to "proper" and what type of discipline in view) are tethered together is because phenomenology aspires to function as a philosophical critique of other disciplines, by which I mean, a critique in the Kantian sense of determining the limitations and constitution – capacity of knowing – of other disciplines. In this function, phenomenology guards against the philosophical over-reach of the natural sciences (to take these disciplines as examples). Yet, this critical service can only function if phenomenology becomes in turn critical towards itself in guarding against the temptation of its own scientific over-reach or encroachment.

The line that demarcates the mutual over-reach of phenomenology as well as the natural sciences is the fundamental issue raised by Husserl under the heading of naturalism. Although the problem of naturalism was central for Husserl's thinking, one could argue that much of the discussion concerning phenomenology and other disciplines today either ignores the complexity of the problem of naturalism or naively promotes a "naturalized" conception of phenomenology. Husserl himself was sensitive to different forms of naturalism (the two forms of naturalism with regard to ideality and naturalism with regard to consciousness were explicitly identified in his celebrated essay "Philosophy as Rigorous Science) as well as the entanglement between naturalism and naiveté. All sciences, and, indeed, all disciplines are necessarily philosophical naive; but as Husserl came to recognize, and at times with difficulty, transcendental phenomenology is haunted by its own form of naiveté. I would suggest that the struggle against naiveté, and not merely against naturalism, characterizes how phenomenology defines itself with regard to other disciplines; if so, it would mean that the relation with other disciplines becomes more complex and, indeed, more fruitful, as exemplified with Merleau-Ponty's phenomenological thought. Setting aside the question of its development from Phenomenology of Perception to the unfinished Visible and the Invisible, a common trait through this transformation is Merleau-Ponty's openness to learning philosophically from other disciplines, whether Gestalt psychology, structural anthropology, linguistics, or contemporary aesthetics. In this latter regard, the beautiful essay Eye and Mind is an example of how phenomenology (in its form as ontological thinking) discovers itself through another mode of thinking, or "discipline," in this case, the paintings of Cézanne. The argument elegantly developed in these pages is the thought that the phenomenological epoché and reduction are only genuinely realized in (Cézanne's) paintings. The discipline of phenomenology must thus learn to see itself in the thought exhibited in paintings and so re-discover a way back to the things themselves ("wild ontology"). In this manner, Merleau-Ponty's own phenomenological analysis of Cézanne's paintings incorporate the same stylistic features of those paintings. The text of *Eye and Mind* is an *ekphrasis* that seeks to become itself a painting in words about a painting in deed. Phenomenological thinking only comes to discover itself properly through the ontological pedagogy of another "discipline." Two consequences of this bold stroke are noteworthy. First, Merleau-Ponty distinguishes between philosophy (as a discourse) and thinking: not every philosophical discourse thinks and, likewise, thinking can occur in other media (painting, literature, etc.). Second, philosophical discourse does not have any proprietary domain over thinking: one must learn to think philosophically through encounters with "non-philosophy." In this way, what we find in other disciplines are provocations to re-discover genuine thinking, often at the price of rejecting established notions in philosophy, including, perhaps, standards ways of conceiving phenomenology itself.

4. What have been the most significant advances in phenomenology?

There are many ways in which one could understand what "significant advance" might mean in philosophy, but since I am skeptical of any conception of "progress" in philosophy (see below), the only way in which I can make sense of such a question is in terms of "advances" measured by two criteria: conceptual fruitfulness and illumining insights. I would like here to single out one problem for which phenomenology has, in my view, been both conceptually fruitfully and genuinely illuminating. I have in mind what I shall simply call the problem of stupidity, which, in my view, is the central problem for Sartre's thinking, and for which his phenomenological analyses of the imaginary, emotions, and bad faith offer a priceless trove of insights. Not that Sartre himself explicitly addresses the phenomenon of stupidity in his writings on the imaginary, emotions, and bad faith, although he does address the topic explicitly in his massive study of Flaubert.

We often meet individuals who strike us as intelligent and stupid. Stupidity is not the opposite of intelligence, but very often its shadow. This raises the question of how a person can be both intelligent, even brilliant, and yet stupid. For Sartre, the problem of stupidity is fundamentally a problem of self-deception, not of intelligence per se. The problem of self-deception here is ontological: it defines a person in their basic manner of being, or existence. Sartre approaches self-deception as rooted in an attitude that we adopt towards the world and ourselves. Implicit in Sartre's analysis of bad faith, emotions, and the imaginary is the insight that stupidity can be understood in terms of what I would call an existential attachment to the importance of what we care about. Indeed, when seen through the prism of Sartre's thinking, the importance of what we care about is liable to become the stupidity of our caring about our own importance. A clue to this analysis is found with the basic metaphors of stupidity—petrification and stubborn closed mindedness—that are central to Sartre's thinking. As seen through Sartre's analysis of bad faith in Being and Nothingness, stupidity can be understood as a condition in which a person has immunized her belief in a certain truth to the claim of any evidence. Rather than considering a belief in a certain truth (the truth of God, the truth of the Nation, etc.) as accountable to the fortunes of the world, a belief is firmly maintained in order not to expose it to the demand of evidence. In this manner, stupidity is form of self-immunization. A person has invested herself fundamentally in a certain truth so as to place this truth and herself beyond the contingency of the world. The mechanism here critically hangs on de-coupling truth from evidence and paradoxically raising truth above evidence. A life thus organized is organized in terms of a desire not to know. Intelligence becomes mobilized in the interest of wanting not to know: hence the cleverness, elusiveness, repetition, aggression, and stubbornness that frequently characterizes our encounters with minds that are closed from the inside. And hence the fundamental tautological recourse of what we hold to be so important: the truth we care so much about holds us firmly in its image at the price of its own meaninglessness and our own self-destructiveness.

5. What are the most important open problems in phenomenology and what are the prospects for progress?

Whether there is anything like progress in philosophy represents one of the crucial philosophical questions that we today massively take for granted. Is not the hubris of our institution this need to believe without every seriously questioning whether "progress" is both philosophically intelligible and desirable? Does philosophical thought today mask its constitutive fragility to the inescapable economic mania for the robustness of productivity—work packages, research impact, publication analytics—through the intoxicating lure and lie of progress? Is there any genuine progress in philosophy? Are philosophical problems of the kind meant to be solved?

These questions define the great contestation between the two visions of phenomenology in Husserl and Heidegger. In Husserl's original form of phenomenological thinking, the possibility and meaningfulness of progress is central to his vision of philosophy and Western history, even as this intellectual confidence in his own project continually underwent critical testing over the course of its development. As Husserl makes plain in the opening sentences of "Philosophy as Rigorous Science", the progress of human reason with regard to its "highest theoretical needs" is essentially an ethical imperative for the advancement of humankind. In this vein, Husserl's understands phenomenology as nothing less than the project of a philosophical modernism. Husserl here announces phenomenology as the advent of a "new science," as the realization of the *telos* of rationality, and most significantly, as promising an ethical-religious realization of genuine humanity—an ethical significance that would become more pronounced in his thinking up until the Crisis. Husserl's idea of phenomenology is wedded to the claim that problems are only meaningful if they can in principle admit of a solution, and in this sense, the uncompromising and indefatigable drive towards clarity under the motto "back to the things themselves" expresses this Husserlian confidence in progress. And yet, essential to Husserl's inauguration of phenomenology was equally a commitment to question the very sense of philosophical questioning. The celebrated method of the phenomenological epoché can in part be seen as a neutralization of inherited ways of questioning philosophically. The movement of reduction represents in this regard a philosophical Bildung or, in other words, a pedagogy of questioning. This procedure of re-minting questions we once thought we knew what it means to ask entails the discovery of new kinds of problems (for example, the central problem of constitution) as much as it requires devising fresh approaches to old problems. The complex development of Husserl's thinking is thus determined by a productive interplay between the doing and undoing of answers in terms of the fashioning and unfashioning of questions. At times, Husserl's proliferation of problems appears Baroque in its countless folds, yet through-out its sinuous course, there reigns a fundamental confidence that progress is possible and, indeed, demanded, for the realization of genuine philosophical thought. In Heidegger, an alternative conception of phenomenological thought comes to fruition, where philosophical thought is foremost not about answering questions but about residing within an attitude questioning that never arrives at itself. Indeed, Heidegger's provocation consists in claiming that questions are essentially in search of themselves. The veritable sense of questioning remains hidden, or forgotten, such that to pursue a question is to endeavor at once its destruction and its renewal. The thrust of Heidegger's thinking can thus be understood as a perpetual insinuation of unknowing at that inaugural moment when we think have mastered what it is to question and hence come into possession of philosophical thought. Whereas, in the case of Husserl, philosophical questioning represents the most complete realization of the autonomy of reason—it is we who question the world—in the case of Heidegger, philosophical thought occurs rarely and under specific circumstances; it is we who are questioned by the world. If questioning ultimately finds its source in us, then confidence in progress with regard to answers is in truth a confidence we place in ourselves. If questioning essentially comes to us, as when we are thrown into questioning, then confidence in progress with regard to answers is in truth a defense against or evasion from allowing ourselves to be questioned in a way that exceeds our mastery—the mastery of our concepts, the mastery of our institutions, the mastery of our discourse—without thereby abrogating our responsibility for questioning.

8

John Drummond

Robert Southwell, S.J. Distinguished Professor of Philosophy and the Humanities

Fordham University (U.S.A.)

---

1. Why were you initially drawn to phenomenology?

Departing home for my undergraduate studies, I had a plan. I was going to study government and the law and then return to my home state of New York and enter politics. This plan was notable for the extraordinary amount of self-deception involved; I simply did not — and do not — have the personality for electoral politics. Thankfully, I was deterred from this plan, not by any reflective insight into my self-deception but, rather, by a philosophy course.

The course in question was required of all students in the College of Arts and Sciences. It was not my first philosophy course. I had previously taken the required courses "Logic" and "Metaphysics," the latter an awful course — a bad instructor combined with material that did not grip my imagination. Serendipity arrived with the next required course in the form of Professor Thomas McTighe, an extraordinary and inspiring teacher who enticed more students, including me, to the study of philosophy than anyone I have known in more than forty years in the profession. The course went by the unfortunate name "Philosophy of Man," a course now generally taught under the names "Philosophy of Human Nature," "Philosophy of the Human," "Philosophy of the Person," or "Philosophical Anthropology". I found myself captivated by the course materials as we explored various answers to questions such as, What is it to be human? How is the human related to the world? and What is the place of the human in that world? This captivation was only heightened in yet another required course "Ethics" organized around responses to the question of what it is to be a *good* human. These were existential issues that thoroughly gripped me. My original plan, although deterred, was not completely derailed, for I also obtained a minor in government. More important, however, I discovered that my interest in politics — even after serving as a national staffer on a presidential campaign in 1968 — had much deeper roots in these questions about what it meant to be human and to be a good human.

Phenomenology was not mentioned in any of these required courses, so what drew me to phenomenology in particular remains an open question. The course of study for the philosophy major at my university was historically organized. As I worked my way through this history, two opposing tendencies manifested themselves. I could never quite get past the thought that Aristotle was a genius, but like many undergraduates, I tended to be convinced by the philosophy I had most recently read, and I read Husserl last! The latter I say mostly in jest, but Husserl's place in the history of philosophy is not of no consequence. What I found in Husserl was in an important way different from — and more attractive than — what I had found in his predecessors.

In lieu of causal or conceptual analyses of concepts such as substance, cause, knowledge, truth, and the like, Husserl and his successors substituted descriptive accounts of different kinds of experience. The existential dimension of this thought again grabbed my attention. Phenomenology certainly had things to say about knowledge and truth, and it certainly had things to say about substance as experienced and cause as experienced. But Husserl's descriptive methodology combined with his notion of the phenomenological reduction offered a new view of what philosophy should be doing and provided a new way to think about philosophical problems. I do not mean to suggest that phenomenology did not address traditional philosophical problems or that it did not appeal to abstract notions of various kinds. Indeed, Husserl, for example, offered a well-developed notion of essences that recalled ancient ideas, and he appealed to a notion of a transcendental ego. All this was in the service, however, of an attempt to *clarify descriptively* the nature of different kinds of experience in a manner that disclosed the *essential structures* of those experiences while addressing and preserving the best features of the traditions that had preceded him.

I left college, then, believing two things: first, Aristotle was probably the smartest person ever to live (Shakespeare was the rival), and, second, that Husserl's extraordinary genius was to retrieve some central features of an Aristotelian approach to philosophy (especially in the radical attention to experience that did not turn empiricistic) while responding to modern objections to Aristotelianism. Those two convictions animated my graduate study, and they continue to animate my work today.

2. What are your main contributions to the field of phenomenology?

My work centers on the notion of intentionality. This should not surprise given my interest in existential questions about the human and human experience. The reflection on experience focuses our attention, first and foremost, on the brute fact that we experience the world at all. Questions about knowledge and truth and even reflective questions about the self who experiences come later. I was struck, in other words, first and foremost by the mind's openness to the world — our "minding" the world — and by the force of Husserl's question of how subjectivity can attain objectivity. There were really two questions here: (1) how does subjectivity attain objectivity in the sense of apprehending an object transcendent to the subject and, (2) how does subjectivity attain objectivity in the sense of experienced objectivity as the shared sense of a community of experiencing subjects.

My dissertation was the first step in my investigation of intentionality. I studied in detail and wrote a critique of Husserl's view of the perception of a material thing in space as presented in his 1907 *Dingkolleg*. I chose this entry point for two reasons: (1) the critical edition of the *Dingkolleg* had just been published, so the material was fresh (and there were few secondary sources — a strategic choice!), and (2) Husserl conceived perception as the founding basis for all other experiences, so this was, in one sense, as fundamental a topic as one could find in the theory of intentionality.

My study of the *Dingkolleg* was undertaken in the light of Aron Gurwitsch's critique of the apprehension/contents-of-apprehension distinction Husserl employed in his account of perceptual acts. The dissertation developed an independent — and, I believe, more phenomenological — criticism of this distinction. The criticism is that the variations by which Husserl supposedly isolates sensation-contents fail to do so. His view attempts to account for the fact that we can experience an unchanging object in differing sensuous appearances and the fact that we can experience different objects in the same sensuous appearance. So, for example, if we change the medium for vision such that we are looking through a fog, an unchanging object will appear less spatially and qualitatively defined. Conversely, his example of the human and the mannequin suggests that the same sensuous appearance can present different objects. Gurwitsch's criticism of the doctrine of presenting sensation-contents was directed toward the second kind of example with its supposed neutrality of sensation-contents to differing perceptual apprehensions. My criticism, by contrast, was directed to the first kind of example. Husserl claimed that given changes in the perceptual organ or the perceptual medium or the subject's mood, the object's *appearance*, but not the object itself, will change. But there is no phenomenological ground for asserting that there are sensation-contents that change as a result of these changes. What is varied is just a set of psycho-physical conditions, and these variations condition and constrain apparent changes in the object because the appearing world and its perceived objects are correlated with both the subject of the perceiving and the conditions under which the perceiving occurs. Some set of these psycho-physical conditions is necessarily present in any perception, although no particular set of them is necessary for a particular perception. The perceptual appearance, then, is not, as Husserl thought, the complex of sensation-contents presenting the objective determinations of the object. Instead, the perceptual appearance (perceptual noema) is the perceived object's appearing under a set of psycho-physical conditions. A change in the appearance of an unchanging object results from a change in one or more of these conditions.

While I accepted Gurwitsch's ontological identification of the noema and object, I rejected his phenomenological account of the relation between noemata and the perceived object. Gurwitsch identifies the object as a whole of presentational parts, and I argue that this is a phenomenological version of phenomenalism. Instead, I argue in the dissertation that the object is a self-transforming identity manifested in and through a manifold of appearances (or, more generally, senses).

Dispensing with the notion of sensation-contents necessitates other modifications in Husserl's phenomenology of perception and his understanding of intentionality. Husserl had postulated a "functional" connection between a flow of kinaesthetic sensations and the flow of sensation-contents such that the flow of sensation-contents is a function of, that is, is motivated by, the flow of kinaesthetic sensations. But this functional connection falls apart once sensation-contents are rejected. Moreover, it is difficult to understand how a flow of kinaesthetic sensations could be said to motivate and constrain a flow of appearances. The proper way to understand the flowing of appearances is as motivated by, or as a function of, the bodily movements themselves such that moving in a particular way both discloses a sequence of appearances and rules out others.

The notion of functional connections is helpful for understanding intentionality in a variety of ways. The motivational connection between bodily activities and perceptual appearances is only one instance of a functional connection. The idea of a functional connection also provides a way to think of the relations between the psycho-physical conditions mentioned above and perceptual appearances. Changes in any one of those conditions motivate and at the same time constrain new appearances of the object.

The account of perception developed in the dissertation raises two other important issues about intentionality. Because Husserl spoke of a relation between two kinds of sensations that he considered real (*reell*) components of a *mental act*, he did not fully appreciate the significance of his appeal to bodily activities. He could continue to think in terms of a pure ego or a transcendental ego apart from its "mundanization." This becomes more difficult, however, when it is the body itself through its movements — rather than some flow of sensations — that is motivating the flow of appearances. The body itself has a functional, constitutive role in perception, and insofar as perception is an ultimately founding experience, we never fully shed our bodyliness and its constitutive role even in higher-order experiences.

This fact necessitates some rethinking of the transcendental character of phenomenology. For example, Husserl's account describes bodily activities — eye movements, say — that are the bodily activities of human perceivers. Other animals, however, are equipped with different sensorimotor systems. Hence, we must ask whether Husserl provides an account of perception as such or only of human perception. Since the bodyliness of perception is carried over into thought insofar as perception is ultimately founding, we must ask whether phenomenology provides an account of rationality as such or an account of human rationality. The possibility of identifying what is essential to rationality as such seems more bound up with and more difficult to distinguish from human rationality. In accordance with this, it becomes more difficult to think of the transcendental in terms of an ego somehow distinct from the psychological ego. This is not to suggest that phenomenology is not a transcendental philosophy, but it is to suggest that it would perhaps make more sense to speak of an irreducible transcendental dimension of the experiencing subject rather than a transcendental ego. To the extent that we experience things as significant for us, we commit ourselves, I believe, to the view that the existence of things is mind-independent but the significance of things is, at least in part, mind-dependent. It is in the disclosure and apprehension of significance that we can locate the transcendental dimension of our experience.

After receiving my degree I turned my attention to the general theory of intentionality. Gurwitsch's account of the relation between noemata and the object they presented was not the only available one. The major alternative was Føllesdal's, and he advanced a view modeled on the relation between ideal species-meanings and expressive acts in Husserl's *Logical Investigations*. His students David Woodruff Smith and Ronald McIntyre presented a similar account, although they modified Føllesdal's view in important ways, bringing it more into line with the correlational view of *Ideas I*. Both accounts viewed the noema as mediating the relation between the intending experience and the intended object. These views, however, conflicted with what I took to be a central feature of the mind's openness to the world. This relation is dyadic, whereas the two views in question conceived it as triadic. Hence, on my view, things not immediately available to reflection and description were inserted into the account. More fundamentally, these views located the intentional reference to the intended object in the noema; hence, an experience was intentional by virtue of its having a noema. This struck me not only as an incorrect interpretation of Husserl, but as an inadequate account of intentionality, which, if it is anything at all, is a characteristic of *mind*, of our *minding the world*.

Others, most notably, Richard Holmes, Robert Sokolowski, and Lenore Langsdorf, had criticized Føllesdal's view, but they either left Gurwitsch's view as the default view because it was the available alternative or I differed with their suggested accounts. Moreover, none of these critiques had dealt with the Smith-McIntyre variation, and I found their view to be importantly different and needing discussion. Hence, along with a critique of these views, I developed a fuller account of what I took to be Husserl's view and introduced modifications to strengthen his general position.

Along the way, I also addressed some higher-level kinds of intentionality and related issues. I have, for example, written on self-awareness and on judgment and logic, including pure formal grammar. Growing out of the work on the perception of material things in space, I offered some views regarding the intentions involved in higher-order views of idealized space. More significantly, perhaps, over the past several years, I have been working on what I sometimes call "moral intentionality," an account of the intentionalities involved in evaluative and volitional experiences.

Here too, while I root my positions in Husserl's, I have developed a phenomenological account that differs in important respects from his. Whereas Husserl speaks of founded acts, I have suggested that the doctrine concerning foundations should be interpreted noematically rather than noetically. Instead of thinking of acts as founding other acts (a kind of piling acts on top of one another), I argue that we should think of our immediate experience of things as perceptual in a broad sense — not merely cognitive but also affective and practical. Husserl suggests this in many places, but his analyses of perception too often address only the cognitive. But if our immediate experience of things is already complex, we should not necessarily think of acts piled on acts, for those immediate experiences have a unity proper to them. Instead of thinking of layers of *acts*, I have suggested that we should think of layers of *sense* in our experience of things as significant. These layers of sense exhibit founding relationships, and I have identified several different kinds of founding relationships at work in evaluative and volitional experience.

In short, I have argued for a view of value-attributes that are disclosed in feelings and emotions and that are dyadic properties that depend in part on the response of a subject with a particular physiological make-up, a particular experiential history, and particular interests, concerns, and commitments. The multiplicity in types of foundational relations undercuts, I believe, the charges of circularity often directed at response-dependence theories. Moreover, the normativity proper to evaluative experiences involves a kind of buck-passing wherein each higher layer of sense finds its justification in the immediately lower level. So practical attributions of right and wrong are justified by appeals to value-attributions concerning ends and actions and agents, and these value-attributions are justified in turn by appeals to non-axiological senses that are justified in the ways appropriate to perceptual and judgmental fulfillment. The fittingness of the motivation of a feeling or emotion and the justification of the axiological sense of the object of the feeling or emotion together constitute the appropriateness of the feeling or emotion. And the appropriateness of the evaluation of the ends sought in action and of the actions undertaken as conducive to those ends constitutes the correctness of practical experience.

In this way, then, I have argued for a kind of eudaimonism that is rooted in the teleological structure of intentionality and Husserl's notion of self-responsibility. My work on moral intentionality touches upon a number of issues in philosophy of mind, most significantly, the emotions and their intentional structure, in meta-ethics, and in normative ethics. These continuing reflections on the various kinds and dimensions of intentionality are my effort to contribute to phenomenological thought. I take intentionality — our directedness, our openness to the world, our experience *of* — to be a brute fact, a basic notion that cannot be analyzed into more fundamental notions. But that does not mean we cannot describe it or that we cannot say many true and interesting things about it!

3. What is the proper role of phenomenology in relation to other disciplines?

This is a complicated issue. Husserl claims that we can have apodictic knowledge of the essential structures of other forms of disciplinary knowledge and of the objects and world as presented in those forms of knowing. He claims also that this philosophical knowledge somehow grounds these other disciplines. But the grounding is not one such that truths in the other disciplines can be deduced from or justified by appeal to philosophical principles. Nevertheless, to the extent that it is true that phenomenology can identify these essential structures, it is also true that phenomenology can, at the least, distinguish science properly understood from "pseudo-science."

Care must be taken, however, even in advancing this claim. In the first place, Husserl acknowledges that even apodictic insights can be overturned, although only by other apodictic insights. The considerations of actual and possible cases that underlie our grasp of essential structures might fail to take into account all the possibilities, especially novel possibilities, for the kind of experience under consideration. It is, for example, generally thought that physics requires experimental confirmations of its claims. But there are recent developments, for example, string theory, that are internally consistent, economical theories but seem not to show promise of experimental predictions that would allow experimental confirmation of the theory. Of course, it might turn out that the theories will eventually yield such predictions, but it might also turn out that they do not. The scientific community, however, because of other advantages of the theories, might decide that one or the other of these theories, despite the absence of experimental predictions in the usual sense, is the preferred theory. It is inconceivable to me that phenomenologists would — or should — insist that the physics accepted by the community of physicists is a pseudo-science. More likely, it seems, is that phenomenologists would have to reconsider the limitations of the variations performed to arrive at their conception of what genuinely constitutes a physical science. This is different from the dubitability and fallibility characteristic of our natural experience, for it would remain the case that the phenomenological philosopher would need apodictic evidence for any new claim advanced.

Second, in disciplines where there is theoretical disunity (and none of the contending theories are deemed pseudo-sciences), the phenomenologist is not capable of deciding between two competing theories. Insofar as it is possible that rival theories could exhibit the essential features of the discipline in question, it is up to the practitioners of the discipline to choose between incommensurable rivals "on balance" and "all things considered." The most a phenomenologist can do is advance a view of what belongs essentially to different disciplines and what it is to be truthful in the different disciplines.

To the extent that phenomenology is a reflection on our minding the world, it has a special relation to the empirical sciences of mind apart from the determination of what essentially characterizes these sciences. I am thinking here especially of psychology and neuroscience. Husserl had spoken of a way through psychology to phenomenology, but I have argued that such talk is misleading. This is only a special instance of the way through ontology. Husserl isolated it because of the common subject matter of phenomenology and psychology and because he thought that what he called "phenomenological psychology" or "intentional psychology" is a way-station on the way to phenomenology. But I think "phenomenological psychology" oxymoronic when thought of as anterior to phenomenology, for once you disclose intentionality as the fundamental structure of mind, you no longer have a psychological science investigating a single region of the world — mind. You have instead a transcendental phenomenology that transcends worldly regions insofar as the intentional correlation encompasses both mind and natural things in the world as significant. A phenomenological psychology posterior to phenomenology is possible insofar as psychology can take up phenomenological findings concerning mind as *disclosive* of the world and apply them to the study of mental events as *in* the world.

This understanding of the relation between phenomenology and the sciences of mind returns us to the question of psycho-physical conditions raised in response to the second question. The (empirical) sciences of mind are well suited to providing an account of these psycho-physical conditions and how they can constrain the appearances of objects and the sense they have for us. Phenomenology, in its notion of psycho-physical conditions, creates a logical space for the empirical sciences of mind in a way that reductivist or physicalist versions of the empirical sciences of mind cannot create the logical space for consciousness and meaning.

4. What have been the most significant advances in phenomenology?

Anyone answering this question is likely to be biased by his or her own areas of research and immediately related areas, and I am no exception. So, I think that phenomenology has made great advances not merely in phenomenology itself but in philosophy in a number of areas. First are foremost are some issues in the philosophy of mind. Phenomenological treatments of intentionality and consciousness (or self-awareness) have great advantages over competing accounts. Phenomenology has explored embodiment in ways unmatched by other philosophical approaches, and this research has led to sophisticated accounts of mind-body issues that expose some of the problems in other contemporary responses to the mind-body problem (which is sometimes reduced to the problem of consciousness). Phenomenology has made important contributions to our understanding of the self and of subjectivity, and it has advanced our understanding of expression, especially linguistic expression, but also artistic expression of various kinds. Finally, phenomenology has advanced our understanding of what an appropriate philosophical methodology ought to be.

5. What are the most important open problems in phenomenology and what are the prospects for progress?

Once again, the answer to this question is going to be determined by one's own philosophical interests and style. I shall mention one problem in phenomenological practice and one problem in phenomenological theory. The practical problem involves a kind of insularity. Too many works in phenomenology do not break outside the circle of phenomenological philosophers. But if we agree that phenomenology has important contributions to make to philosophy as such, phenomenologists should address their work to a larger philosophical audience. This requires that we engage philosophical views developed through different, non-phenomenological approaches and explore how a phenomenological approach can address the lacunae and problems that exist in those other approaches. And, of course, we will sometimes learn from those approaches such that we can improve our phenomenological accounts.

The area I wish to focus on is ethics, and what I shall say picks up the spirit of the previous remark. There has certainly been a great deal of work done in ethics from a phenomenological perspective. At the same time, however, these discussions have often remained "internal" to the phenomenological and continental traditions. But phenomenology has, I think, a great deal of interest to say about meta-ethics and moral psychology by way of analyzing the intentionalities involved in valuation and volition. Moreover, what it can say in response to these problems has implications for normative ethics. So, I think it would be good for phenomenologists to engage issues regarding moral realism, quasi-realism, neo-sentimentalism, and sensibility views in meta-ethics, and I think it would be good for phenemenologists to indicate how the normative implications of a phenomenological ethics bear on other major normative theories, in particular, deontologism, consequentialism, and virtue ethics. The good news is that with the resurgence of forms of Kantian constructivism and both consequentialist and eudaimonistic approaches to virtue theory, there is ample opportunity to bring phenomenological descriptions to the consideration of these normative alternatives.

9

Günter Figal

Professor of Philosophy
University of Freiburg (Germany)

---

1. Why were you initially drawn to phenomenology?
Already at school Heidegger's *Being and Time* and some writings of Sartre came to my hands, and as a student, motivated mainly by Michael Theunissen, with whom I worked especially closely in these years, I also read Husserl – *Cartesian Meditations, Ideas I*, the *Crisis* book and also, quite intensely, the manuscripts on phenomenology of intersubjectivity. It took some time however till I discovered phenomenology as my way of philosophical thinking. My dissertation was on Adorno's aesthetics and thus deeply embedded in dialectical philosophy. But apparently my dialectical training had not been all too formative since dialectics became more and more dubious for me. As I suspected dialectics could do well without particular objects as a challenge for thinking and thus without descriptive attempts. So for dialectical philosophers like Hegel and Adorno art in general is much more important than are particular artworks; particular works that appear in their writings often are assimilated to their theory. My experience as a student of literature and as an aficionado of paintings and music was different; by experience I learned that artworks require attention to their individuality, close reading, hearing or beholding, and detailed interpretation. It was Gadamer, as a teacher and as the author of *Truth and Method,* who showed me that and, to some degree, how such attitudes can be reflectively described and thus be discovered as a philosophical topic. So because of my devotion to art I was drawn into hermeneutics, and I was so much absorbed by hermeneutical topics and questions that I only additionally realized that hermeneutics must be understood as a specification of phenomenology. Phenomenology was always present, but more as a kind of ground or even background for my attempts to find my way in philosophy.

It was only after I had moved from the University of Tübingen to the University of Freiburg that I had a concrete idea of how to conceive hermeneutics phenomenologically. More and more I had realized that hermeneutical experience should not or at least not only be understood in the way Gadamer understands it, namely as the process of effective history. If understanding is conceived only as a twofold manifestation of meaning, meaning as presupposed by the experiencing person and meaning as becoming manifest in the process of experience, the dependency of understanding on something that claims understanding cannot sufficiently be taken into account. But there really are hermeneutical objects that readers and interpreters refer to; objects, which are not absorbed by the process of understanding, but which, as solid structures, can initiate this process again and again. So, again, hermeneutical experience is not just a process in Gadamer's sense, but rather belongs into a phenomenal correlation, in which something, namely a hermeneutical object, shows itself in understanding whereas understanding realizes the self-showing of such an object in realizing a complex of its possibilities to be understood. Conceived in this way the subject matter of hermeneutics is the interplay between interpretative attempts to understand and objects to be understood, between self-showing and interpretative representation.

This interplay however cannot sufficiently be described if only its two correlates are taken into account. The interplay requires an openness, in which it can take place, an openness, which I call in my book *Gegenständlichkeit*, translated as *Objectivity*, the hermeneutical space of freedom, language and time. Only in this space hermeneutical objects can show themselves so that they can be experienced in their appearance. Thus in attempting to clarify the structure of hermeneutic experience I came upon phenomenal structures and upon phenomenality itself.

For an answer to the question of how the openness for the interplay between understanding and its objects can be conceived, I could integrate a topic that had been decisive for me since the years after I had finished my dissertation and that proved to be decisive for my conception of phenomenology in general. After my dissertation I had become interested in the topic of freedom, not just freedom of action or freedom of the will, but freedom as an essential character of human life. As a consequence my attention had been drawn to Schelling's *Investigations of Human Freedom* as well as to Kierkegaard's *Sickness to Death*, but also, again, to Heidegger's *Being and Time*. It was Heidegger's book, which finally absorbed all my attention, and so the book I wrote was mainly devoted to it. What had intrigued me mostly in this context was Heidegger's understanding of freedom as free space (*Freiraum*), as a realm of the possible that particular decisions and activities or passivities are embedded in. Freedom, understood as the openness of the possible in this way is prior to decisions and activities and never exhausted by them. My book, entitled *Martin Heidegger. Phänomenologie der Freiheit* was my first contribution to phenomenology. In character however it was not primarily systematic, but a close reading mainly of *Being and Time* and a critical examination of Heidegger's argument. I stressed Heidegger's discovery of freedom as openness, but I did not yet know how to make this discovery phenomenologically productive. When I learned over the years how to do this I also, step by step, developed what I would call my main contribution to phenomenology.

2. What are your main contributions to the field of phenomenology?

When Heidegger speaks of openness (*Offenheit*) or clearing (*Lichtung*), of horizon (*Horizont*) or region (*Gegend*) he cannot avoid evoking associations to spatiality though he does not understand his terms as referring to space. Heidegger never developed a sufficiently detailed conception of space, neither in *Being and Time,* nor in his later writings. One could regard this just as a blind spot in his philosophical work. But one could also go beyond Heidegger's philosophical project and ask whether the openness, in which beings can be experienced, could be understood more concretely and also more adequately if conceived as space. If, furthermore, the experience of beings could be understood as reference to something that shows itself and thus as to phenomena, space would be openness for phenomenality.

Considerations like these have led me to a conception of spatial phenomenology, which I have elaborated in my book *Unscheinbarkeit. Der Raum der Phänomenologie*. According to this book phenomena as such are spatial; their phenomenality is their spatiality. And as a consequence phenomenology as such has to be a reflection and description of space; understanding phenomena as such, i.e. phenomenologically then is tantamount to reflecting and describing them in their spatiality.

This general assumption may sound plausible in certain respects, but it may also be regarded as disputable. Admittedly, living beings as well as things and mostly buildings can certainly not be described adequately without taking into account their spatial character. Living beings that move do so spatially and in space; perception is spatial, since colors, sounds, odors or scents and also the correlates of tactile experience are only accessible spatially. The same holds true for things that can be examined in their extension from different sides and that can be nearer by or farer away. Buildings, rooms built for habitation or visit, are essentially built space, and as such they are more or less obvious. But even if this is so, why should one favor space in such a way as to conceive it as enabling phenomenality? Why space and not time, which had been so prominent for Husserl and Heidegger, or at least space *and* time, in accordance with a quasi symmetrical understanding of both, which very likely can be traced back to Kant's transcendental aesthetics in his *Critique of Pure Reason?*

There are good reasons for not following Husserl and Heidegger as in their phenomenological preference for time. One can show in detail that the spatiality of entities or events constitutes their phenomenality, whereas they are temporally only ordered in their phenomenality. Something can only be determined as 'earlier' or 'later' than something else or as being 'present', 'past' or 'in the future' if it is or was or will be *somewhere*. The same holds true for events, which, in order to be events at all, must take *place* or must have taken place somewhere. On the other hand one can speak of something being or happening at a certain place without positioning it in a temporal order. It may happen or have happened or will be happening in the future and nevertheless be regarded as the same event, whereas something being nowhere cannot be an entity or an event at all.

One may add to these considerations that Husserl's – and thereby also Heidegger's – preference of time over space is not just a consequence of phenomenological analysis but rather a presupposition necessary for Husserl's conception of phenomenology. As Husserl assumes phenomena are primarily 'subjective' phenomena; as phenomena they belong to the 'immanent being' of consciousness, instead of being regarded as something, which is 'really' there and in its reality 'transcendent'. In the immanent sphere of consciousness however everything is mainly constituted in the temporal flow and by the temporal order of consciousness as such, which, as Husserl states in *Ideas I* in order to be does not need any external being. But on the other hand Husserl knew very well that the correlates of intentional attitudes couldn't be conceived without taking into account their 'transcendence'. And, as one should add, it must be 'real' transcendence, 'real' externality, instead of being just consciously stated; for it can only be truly stated if it is, what it is, namely 'real' transcendence. As a consequence of these considerations neither Husserl's transcendental ego nor Heidegger's *Dasein* can any longer function as the fundament of phenomenology; phenomena as such are not dependent on 'subjective' constitution in whatsoever sense, and thus they are no internal features of transcendental egos or individual instantiations of *Dasein*.

This is a sketch of a conception of phenomenology, which is also meant as a phenomenological conception of realism – a conception taking the external character of phenomena seriously and also doing justice to the fact that reality is only accessible as something experienced. If investigated phenomenologically however reality must be different from reality as experienced in the attitudes of everyday life; it must be obvious in its phenomenal character, i.e. in its showing itself.

But what does this mean? What *is* self-showing or phenomenality? An answer to this question can be given in describing how something shows itself and how it can show itself. One will soon find out that this cannot be done without essentially taking into account the spatiality of the entities in question. This spatiality can be described more or less in detail, but one may find at least three characters of space, which prove to be indispensable. Something shows itself at a particular *place*, in a *free space*, which allows its self-showing in particular way, and it shows itself in its *extension*, which also includes its distance from other entities so that there is space between something and something else. Something can *show* itself at a place, in free space and being extended, external of something else because place, free space and interspace normally do not draw attention. They do not appear, without being concealed or withdrawn. They are inconspicuous; they are to be experienced only along with the phenomena they allow being what they are.

The enabling character of space can be described more in particular, whereupon this particularity proves to be dependent on the character of what is enabled. The self-showing of things is different from that of buildings, which both are different from the self-showing of living beings. And different again is the spatiality of living beings, insofar as they are showing themselves mainly as experiencing the self-showing of something. This dependency of space as enabling on what is enabled gives evidence of its character as enabling. Space is no principle one could refer to, no solid ground on which phenomena could be based. But it is just as little pure openness that withdraws as soon as one makes attempts to describe it. Space is openness that can be described along with what is spatial. Accordingly these descriptions can be reflected as elucidations of the phenomenal interplay between phenomena and their inconspicuous enabling.

3. What is the proper role of phenomenology in relation to other disciplines?

Descriptive phenomenology as I understand it is not exclusive. It has no particular realm of description as has Husserl's phenomenology, which is devoted to the immanence of pure consciousness and thereby is pure phenomenology, whereas, according to Husserl, every reference to something real and transcendent belongs to the 'natural attitude'. Realistic phenomenology in my sense shares the reality it describes with non-phenomenological ways of experience and description; what only makes the difference is that phenomenological description is initiated and led by the reflection of phenomenality. This reflection functions as a kind of index, which gives descriptions a different status and often also a different style – more conceptual than other descriptions, and, first of all, essentially attentive to phenomenality. Nevertheless phenomenological descriptions are necessarily embedded in the context of considerations and descriptions, which are not phenomenological. E.g. the attempt to conceive aesthetics phenomenologically as elaborated in my book *Erscheinungsdinge,* translated as *Aesthetics as Phenomenology,* does not – and cannot – only include original phenomenological conceptions and arguments. Phenomenological thinking necessarily refers to philosophical thinking, which is not phenomenological, and also to investigations and descriptions, which are scientific or belong to the humanities or are even poetic texts. Phenomenology as I understand it inscribes its descriptions in various discourses; it integrates various insights and elucidations and it thus requires capacities and experiences, which are not originally phenomenological.

Such an understanding of phenomenology makes it difficult to determine its relation to other disciplines. Phenomenology is no separate discipline that could interact with others; it is no homogenous formation of research but has always already been formed by conceptions and experiences different from it. This does not mean however that phenomenology has no profile of its own. Its profile is constituted by its proper question, namely the question how phenomenality can be conceived and described. Phenomenological thinking is only what it should be with the reflection of phenomenality. This reflection is indispensable; otherwise phenomenology is at risk of dissolution even if the label 'phenomenology' is maintained. Such dissolution may happen if e.g. a scientific discourse dominates an inquiry meant as 'phenomenological', but also if subject matters traditionally belonging to phenomenology, like alterity or embodiment, are discussed without a clear conception of phenomenality. Phenomenological investigations are really phenomenological if all concepts and descriptions belonging to them illustrate or explain a particular understanding of what phenomena are and of how they can be experienced as such. Only phenomenology that truly is what it should be could be productive for sciences and humanities and also for non-academic discourses. And only then phenomenology can avoid presuppositions, which make its investigations opaque or even jeopardize its philosophical character; philosophy without the claim to avoid presuppositions is no philosophy at all. Even if this claim can never totally be fulfilled it characterizes philosophy in its attempt not only to think conceptually but, in doing so, also to clarify its concepts; also to take nothing describable for granted, but to develop descriptions as if they were developed for the first time. In such a way philosophical thinking is guided by wonder, which, according to Aristotle, is the origin of philosophy as such.

4. What have been the most significant advances in phenomenology?

Since the publication of Husserl's *Logical Investigations* more than a hundred years ago phenomenology has developed impressively. One only has to recall the names of philosophers like Heidegger, Merleau-Ponty, Sartre and Levinas as well as to think of the lively international phenomenological scene of today to draw the conclusion that phenomenology has been established as one of the major philosophical movements of our time. During a hundred years of phenomenology Husserl's groundbreaking discoveries have been refined and differentiated; the potential of phenomenological analysis and description has been extended, and topics not phenomenologically pertinent for Husserl himself have been discovered, topics, which today have proved to be integral elements of the phenomenological field. As to the latter one may think of Gadamer's philosophical hermeneutics or, even more, of Merleau-Ponty's considerations on painting, which have initiated a completely new way of philosophical aesthetics and also deeply influenced the theory of the visual arts. In order to illustrate the actual significance of phenomenological thinking one could also mention the increasing interest in a phenomenological version of philosophy of mind. In sum, there is sufficient evidence that phenomenology has a promising future if philosophy as such has a future at all; philosophy however will not be able to do without conceptual descriptions of ourselves and of the world that cannot be replaced by results of scientific research. So phenomenology can be supportive to philosophy in general; in order to survive philosophy probably needs to be phenomenological.

Whatever phenomenology has already contributed and will continue to contribute to philosophy and to our understanding of the world in general, there is good reason to assume that the most important achievement of phenomenology is phenomenology itself. The discovery that initiated phenomenology as such has been a decisive philosophical step, and it has been a modest one, without cultural or political, much less revolutionary ambitions. When Husserl in *Ideas I,* articulates the conviction "that everything that offers itself to us originally in 'intuition' (in its corporeal actuality, so to speak) is to be accepted simply as what it is presented as being", he tacitly abandons the classical distinction between 'mere phenomena' and 'true beings' as it was established by Plato or, rudimentarily, already by Parmenides. According to Husserl's "principle of principles" true beings are phenomena as well as are indications or deceptive appearances. Everything whatsoever has to be taken in its accessibility, and things really accessible are 'the real things'. There is nothing 'behind' the accessibility of something for us; there are only always other ways of accessibility; our intentions, perceptions and cognitions are no illusions or mere constructions, but really make accessible what can be accessible. And as to the character of things accessible there is no longer an ontological hierarchy, in which the intelligible is favored over the perceptible. How the intelligible and the perceptible is to be assessed depends on the particular phenomena in question. There may be a dominance of eidetic aspects or a dominance of the aesthetical. Painters, especially modern painters, have shown impressively how an exploration of the visible that is not subordinate to the intelligible can be achieved.

Accordingly the phenomenological project is essentially open-minded. There is nothing to be excluded from the realm of phenomenological interest, and this has always been one of the advantages of phenomenology. Prominent phenomenological achievements have often been true explorations of topics that have not found philosophical attention before. As an illustration one could refer to Husserl's description of kinesthetic experience or, again, to Merleau-Ponty's discussion of painting. And Sartre, with his descriptions of being regarded and observed by others, has discovered aspects of human life unknown in the field of social philosophy before.

5. What are the most important open problems in phenomenology and what are the prospects for progress?

To speak of 'open problems' includes that at least some problems are solved. These problems must not bother scholars any longer so that they concentrate on the open problems and try to solve them. Philosophical questions are not of this kind. Though there are real discoveries in philosophy none of these discoveries can be regarded as being realized once and for all. In the contrary, the most advancing discoveries need to be restated, reformulated and re-interpreted, again and again; one has to rediscover them and thus find one's own philosophical way. So in philosophy the most important discoveries never vanish, and accordingly there can never be what Heidegger dreamt of in the thirties: a completely new beginning. Philosophy has no absolute beginning and no end; who begins to philosophize finds herself or himself always already in the middle of philosophy. In this situation some problems appear to be open, namely the problems, which have just initiated philosophical thinking. Philosophical problems are not open for everyone, but rather for philosophers who regard them as their open problems, as the questions they wish to understand, to ask as clearly as possible, and to answer.

So what are my open problems? There are many particular ones, which have emerged from my conception of spatial, realistic phenomenology. One of them is the problem how the character of something that is essentially a particular space, but not a built space or room, can be conceived and described. An exhibited collection of pictures e.g. is a space, namely the space of an exhibition, in which every picture has its particular place value and in which every picture can only be experienced in the context of others. This 'context' indicates what may be called the space of the exhibition. Such a space surely cannot be experienced without a room or an ensemble of rooms in a building. But it is not identical with this room or ensemble of rooms; the exhibition could be removed and be reinstalled at another place, and still it would be the same exhibition.

The problem as sketched goes beyond examples like the one just given. What e.g. is the "space of reasons" Wilfrid Sellars speaks of in his essay *Empiricism and the Philosophy of Mind*? Is it a 'real' space or is it only metaphorically called 'space'? What, in the latter case, would be the *tertium comparationis* that would allow the metaphorical use of the word 'space'? But if the space of reasons is a real space, how then can it be conceived and described? One can show that for human beings space as it is bodily experienced is also conceptually structured; I have made attempts to show this in the last chapter of *Unscheinbarkeit*. Does this lead to the conclusion that the space of intelligibility is conceived as space in orientation to space as experienced kinesthetically? Or can we speak of space in such an all-encompassing sense that space as such includes the intelligible and the perceptible so that it makes the intelligible to be intelligible like it enables the perceptible to be perceived?

Maybe the elaboration of these questions and the answers I can find for them will prove to be only a number of footnotes to my book. But there is at least one other 'open problem', which in the book is only touched upon and which will need further extensive examination, namely the problem of what I would like to call 'spatial normativity'. If space enables the phenomenal, the showing itself of whatever as well as the different modes of experiencing self-showing, then space, as enabling, would also let the orientation to self-showing be obliging. The experience of openness and thus of space would be the original experience of truth, and Husserl's "principle of principles" would not only be the *magna charta* of phenomenology, but also a kind of categorical imperative. Is phenomenology as such normative, so that the quest for a special phenomenological ethics would be dispensable? And if this would be so – how could the normativity of phenomenology also cover the norms of individual and social life? Is philosophy as such the paradigm of good life, as Plato thought, or do we need a separate philosophical investigation of how to live one's life, an 'ethical' one in Aristotle's sense, which discusses philosophy and philosophical life only exoterically, from the outside?

9. Günter Figal

As to a very sketchy and preliminary answer to this question, much can be said in favor of the assumption that the quest for truth is not just one norm among others but the ethically fundamental one. What we call 'bad' or 'evil' has essentially to do with falseness and deception. Truth, phenomenologically conceived as openness and thus as space, then would also be the key to ethics and to genealogy of morals. In any case it will be truth realized not at least in the responsibility of reasoning. Space as such then might prove to be the space of reasons so that we human beings, who are not only in space, but live space with every experience we make, also live space in responsibility.

10

Shaun Gallagher

Lillian and Morrie Moss Professor of Excellence
University of Memphis (U.S.A.)

---

1. Why were you initially drawn to phenomenology?
My initial interest in phenomenology came by reading the existentialist philosophers during my undergraduate studies. Sartre especially. When I went on to graduate school I wanted to know about the sources that Sartre had been using, so that led me to Hegel, Husserl and Heidegger. I became very interested in the problem of time-consciousness, and did my Masters thesis on that topic, focusing on Husserl's account. For my PhD project I focused more on Merleau-Ponty and embodiment, but still had my interest in temporality. So my dissertation was on embodiment and temporality in phenomenology. Influenced by Merleau-Ponty I also studied the neuroscience and psychology literatures on these topics and took graduate seminars in these disciplines.

2. What are your main contributions to the field of phenomenology?
I keep writing about time. My 1998 book, *The Inordinance of Time*, was about the phenomenology of time in James, Husserl and a number of other phenomenologists. Several years before publishing that book I attended a week-long workshop at King's College, Cambridge. I was the lone phenomenologist in a mix of analytic philosophers of mind, psychologists, neuroscientists, and anthropologists. From that time onward I developed an interest in the cognitive sciences as an interdisciplinary approach to the mind. Given my previous work, my focus was on embodied cognition and the neuroscience and psychology side, rather than AI. Just before my book on time was published I met Francisco Varela, and his work really reinforced my study of embodied cognition, especially from the enactivist perspective. This fit nicely with my interest in Merleau-Ponty's work.

Most of my work, then, has been in the area of embodied cognition, inspired primarily by Merleau-Ponty. I've tried to show how phenomenology is relevant to cognitive science and especially to the more embodied and enactive approaches to cognitive science. My work with

Dan Zahavi is in this area. It covers a number of topics, and I've done a lot of work on the notions of action, intentionality, and agency. I've also explored what such approaches can say about psychopathology, where the sense of agency, and various aspects of self break down.

3. What is the proper role of phenomenology in relation to other disciplines?

I've spent a lot of time thinking about phenomenology in relation to the cognitive sciences, and I've written a lot about methodology, about Varela's notion of neurophenomenology, and my own conception of front-loaded phenomenology. My most recent work has been on defending a non-reductionist approach to cognitive science, and I think phenomenology plays an important role here and can provide a way to keep first-person experience in the mix of things that are relevant for the sciences that usually try to reduce it to third-person data. My new book, *A Neurophenomenology of Awe and Wonder*, is a good example of this approach. It's written with a research team that includes neuroscientists, psychologists, art historians, philosophers and simulation engineers. We conducted experiments that integrated these disciplines in order to study first-person experiences of awe and wonder during space travel. The focus was on the experiences had by over 100 subjects who spent time in a virtual reality simulation of space travel to see if we could replicate the experiences described by astronauts during space flight. Here phenomenology was absolutely essential as part of our methodology. But we also were able to record brain processes by EEG and fNIR, monitor heart rate, and correlate all of that with the first-person descriptions of experiences during the simulations, and data about each subject's cognitive skill level and cultural background (explored through a series of questionnaires). This is, we argue, a way to do non-reductionist cognitive science, using a pluralistic, "large" methodology, and focusing quite a bit on how to integrate everything.

So, on my view, phenomenology can work with other disciplines. It always has, in fact. One finds phenomenology in medical disciplines, clinical psychology and psychiatry, and more recently in physical therapy, and working with patients with cerebral palsy, Parkinson's Disease, and so on. I can give you recent references to this kind of interdisciplinary work. Most of these involve therapeutic applications of phenomenology. But I think that with philosophers and scientists like Merleau-Ponty and Varela, we find ways to use phenomenology in experimental research.

4. What have been the most significant advances in phenomenology?

I'll say something controversial here. Not everyone will agree, and it may not be true from all perspectives. When I was in graduate school I was very interested in phenomenology. But the growing trend was post-phenomenology, post-structuralism, post-modernism, and so forth – a lot of which was critical of Husserl and the phenomenologists, even as these movements built on some aspects of phenomenology. It seemed that phenomenology, in the philosophical arena, was really on its way out; a lot of philosophers were abandoning ship, trading their Husserliana for deconstruction, and so forth, and most of the work in phenomenology that I was familiar with was really a kind of historical scholarship – *looking back* on what Husserl meant about this or that, or how Heidegger related to Husserl, or how Sartre did what he did, and so forth. It was all looking back. One exception was Dreyfus, although everyone I knew complained about his interpretation of Husserl. But at least Dreyfus was looking forward. So I think that the most significant advances in phenomenology in recent times have been the advances of phenomenology into the area of the cognitive sciences, and especially embodied cognition. And that too has been driving new phenomenological work in clinical psychiatry, medicine, and the other areas I mentioned. So when I was in graduate school the future of phenomenology looked quite bleak; in the past 25 years or so, however, the way that many people are using phenomenology has become extremely exciting.

5. What are the most important open problems in phenomenology and what are the prospects for progress?

There is a lot of consternation about whether phenomenology can be naturalized. I don't think this is a major issue myself, but a number of people do. I think that anyone who wants to continue the transcendental project can and should do so. The employment of phenomenology in the natural sciences of mind is a different project that expands the horizons of phenomenology in a productive way. In this regard, no one is proposing that we replace transcendental phenomenology with a naturalized phenomenology. One open and important problem, however, is how precisely to define this naturalization, and part of that question involves the idea that we need to rethink the concept of nature. There is an obvious difference between the idea of naturalizing phenomenology on the assumption that science has already provided the proper concept of nature, and the idea of a phenomenology that engages with science in a way that challenges that very conception of nature. I think that Evan Thompson, for example, is doing some excellent work on this issue.

Another related issue, I think, is to sort out how phenomenology relates to enactivism. I find myself using the phrase 'enactive phenomenology' with only a vague sense of what that means. But I think that there are important synergies between enactivist conceptions of embodied cognition and phenomenology – this can be seen even in the historical connections between Merleau-Ponty and the enactivist approach, but this stretches back to Husserl's notion of the 'I can', as well as Heidegger's notion of *Zuhandenheit*. There are enactivists, however, who merely pay lip service to these phenomenological connections, and I think phenomenologists have to make clear that you don't really get enactivism without these connections. I, myself, have pointed out that the pragmatists are also important for enactivism in this regard, but I think phenomenology is even more directly tied to the development of the enactivist approach. Given that enactivism remains controversial and the subject of continuing critiques from more traditional cognitivist, internalist, and reductionist cognitive science, I think the appeal to the rich phenomenological tradition remains relevant – indeed, the way I would put it is that phenomenologists who are so inclined should enter into these debates to support, or enhance, or to transform enactivism so that it can deliver on its promise to provide a radical rethinking of the way we think about the mind.

Finally, I would recommend that we all get over what has been an entirely unproductive divide between phenomenology and analytic philosophy of mind. This is something that philosophers on both sides need to do. In this regard, I would say that we need to look to the historical roots of both phenomenology and analytic philosophy, look to those areas in which we share some vocabulary, those areas where we do agree, and then engage in a healthy debate about our disagreements, centered on issues, and without the active or passive aggressive behaviors that really don't make philosophical sense. In saying this, I acknowledge that there are political issues that motivate much of the antagonism, but in the larger world, and even in the larger academic world, such motivations reflect a small-minded politics.

11

Miguel García-Baró

Professor of Philosophy

Chairman, Department of Philosophy, Humanities and Communication

Universidad Pontificia Comillas, Madrid (Spain)

---

1. Why were you initially drawn to phenomenology?

In my last years as an undergraduate philosophy student at Universidad Complutense (Madrid), I took part in a seminar conducted by Dr. Juan Miguel Palacios, who had studied with Gottfried Martin and was a direct intellectual heir of the phenomenologists and Kantians that had suffered, here in Madrid, the consequences of the Spanish Civil War (1936-1939), José Ortega y Gasset and Manuel García Morente especially. Palacios, and my own family too, also had a profound connection with Miguel de Unamuno, the Spanish thinker I most admired at that time. Our research back then dealt with the Kantian Critics, while paying especial attention to the problems of the already imminent renewal of democratic life in Spain, following Ortega's liberal ideas.

As part of our principles for national renovation, the need to distance my own work from the uses of the much-impoverished Spanish university (I'm referring to the 1970-1975 period) was imposed on me. The question that appealed to me the most was the analysis of the problem of truth, considered from the perspective of the method with which the *Kritik der reinen Vernunft* was thought and written. I found there a circular argument that puzzled me: transcendental logic seemed to be based on formal logic, and *vice versa*. It was then that Palacios acquainted me with Husserl's *Formale und transzendentale Logik*, and advised that I should travel to Mainz to meet Gerhard Funke, known Husserlian successor of Martin at the direction of the *Kant-Studien*. A scholarship from DAAD made it possible for me to stay in Mainz for two years of very intense activity. (During which I was also introduced to the departments of Catholic Theology and, most importantly, Greek Philology – I very much admired Walter Nikolai.)

I worked at that time on the recently edited volumes *Zur Phänomenologie der Intersubjektivität*, and in workshops in which Kierkegaard, Heidegger and Husserl's lessons *Erste Philosophie* were principal matters of study. I also received help in my work from the late Wilhelm Teichner.

Upon my return to Spain in 1978, I immediately started teaching as an assistant professor in the Logic Department of Universidad Complutense and began a series of lectures on the *Logische Untersuchungen* while at the same time lectured on Plato's *Socratic* dialogues.

A workgroup was quickly set up which devoted itself to Phenomenology. I prompted the Mexican-Spanish publisher Fondo de Cultura Económica to resume the translation of Husserl's works by publishing with them the first version of *Die Idee der Phänomenologie* (1982). Then I brought my attention back to Husserlian transcendental logic until the completion of my doctoral thesis (1983), *Crítica de la razón lógica* (whose essential parts were all covered and extended in my initial book from 1993: *La verdad y el tiempo*). The workgroup that had been formed by then has never dissolved. It has been, in one way or another, the origin of most of my later works.

But I still have not mentioned the deepest reason why I was drawn to phenomenology. It is that only in phenomenology could I find a Socratism strong enough to match our times, and I was convinced that philosophy could only find its own path under the sign of the Socratic. My own original contact with existence revealed in it a quality of adventure towards the unknown, which clashed with the pedantic Kantian-like systems, and also with monism of any kind whatsoever (whether the rationalist denial of freedom or the empiricist atomization of the self). What is real, as a correlate of human life, presents a quality of singularity and novelty, poses a challenge so constant and so deep to a strong subjectivity which is already real as well, that truth does not let us display itself as schematic and frozen in fixed shapes. Philosophy cannot account for truth by forcing it into neat tables of concepts but only by ways of an inexhaustible richness of detail in its description, by artistically matching emotions and words with the inexhaustibly rich. From the beginning of my commitment to philosophy I could see that its figure should definitely, at least for me, favor the *a posteriori* – what is discovered through action and search and openness towards events – over the *a priori*.

In my personal case, not only some decisive experiences (a vivid intimacy with death and gloominess during childhood, later with absolute hope, and even later with love and wretchedness and guilt), but also parallel studies on Literature and Philology, as well as a deep interest towards Judaism and Christianity, all predisposed me to long for another kind of philosophy, more suited to the thirst for reality that I felt: one adopting a narrative form, while committed to follow an absolute imperative of responsibility and good. Although without concepts, as a child everyone of us grasped the difference between that what should be considered *a mystery* and that what is just *a problem*. It is *mysterious* the brief and irreversible condition of the time we have to live; it is *mysterious* that perfect joy and good should have an ineffable, unimaginable, perhaps even unthinkable quality. All the rest is just problematic, interesting; at most, it is paradoxical, an enigma.

The experience that inserts one's life in time is the discovery that *I myself* want neither death nor this life to be definitive – and that ultimately no one does either; that the very alternative between *to be* and *not to be* is already unlivable. Initially, one does not know *what* to look for as the perfect Good, but indeed experiments the need of a *patience* which would let the course of life itself develop towards its mysterious maturity, with that mysterious care that shows each of our lives; by gradually unveiling the significance of the mystery of an existence in tension towards the unknown and the seemingly unthinkable.

Phenomenology showed me that these existence-founding experiences are not matters just to be left to art and religion, but may and must be integrated in philosophical thought. A philosophy that does not integrate them remains a mere reflection on sciences or the structure of language, but cannot provide real understanding or shed light on existence. And in philosophy it is imperative to strive for clarity, to respect the differences between what can be said and what is ineffable; and, most importantly, to commit the personal existence fully to the service of responsibility and the good. For clarity, responsibility and good go necessarily together, despite the long history of criticism that this evident claim has so often received.

Those who are taking their first steps in philosophy, who already live in this situation of radical schism between the unavoidable attention to the problems of existence and the constant and almost secret concern about its mysteries, urge to know about themselves, and also to analyze the ways in which they inhabit truth; and then later they will need to complete their knowledge about nature, history and society. But always from the perspective of the love for detail and the unexpected, imprinted on them by the phenomenological method.

We philosophize out of *shame*, Levinas has very properly stated; and there extends between Philosophy and broad strokes, or Philosophy and the disregard for good, an infinite distance.

2. What are your main contributions to the field of phenomenology?

From the standpoint of the history of thought and the Spanish university, I was involved in the first moments of the renewal of the interest towards Husserl in my country. The seminar *Fenomenología y filosofía primera* has been, for almost 40 years now, a real paradise for all who have integrated it. Not only my books, but also those of many of the best current Spanish philosophers, have been contrived there (I will only mention Agustín Serrano de Haro, Pilar Fernández Beites, Manuel Abella, Andrés Simón, Víctor Tirado, Mariano Crespo, Olga Belmonte e Iván Ortega).

My hermeneutical work on the texts of Husserl has focused on the *Logische Untersuchungen*, of which I am able to present a quite finished interpretation, which has ended up differing notably from the most common and popular ones. I exposed mostly on the course of my translation and comment of the first version of this book, in which whole paragraphs appear, of the utmost theoretical relevance, which were suppressed in following editions but are the precise ones, which hold the key to an understanding of the original text. Until now only the volume devoted to *Prolegomena zur reinen Logik* has been found, but we can already appreciate the global meaning of this interpretation, which, on the other hand, points out the necessity to introduce such a concept of the immediate object as the one Husserl some years later so unfortunately named *noema*.

My interpretation presents the *Logische Untersuchungen* fully within the purposes of the school of Brentano, although in deep divergence with him. It shows that representationalism is not radically surpassed (the *primäre Inhalte* are interpreted as *Abschattungen*, that is to say, as projections of primary qualities from the things of the real-empirical world); that the notion of a general ontology as mereology (brought even into the analysis of the *inneres Zeitbewusstsein*) is in conflict with the possibility of interpreting phenomenology as a first philosophy; that a confidence in the theologically-based realism of Brentano plays a decisive role in the theoretical basis of this book; that intentionality, in virtue of the peculiar and inadequate *distinctio phaenomenologica* which Husserl elaborates (V *Logische Untersuchungen*), is only conceived as instantiation; that, despite the harsh direct criticisms to John Locke, the proximity to a way of thinking similar to his is still very remarkable; and that the *intentionale Materie* comes directly from the passive association of *primary contents*.

Since the doctrine of the *Essenz* turns out to be absurd – so is, in general, the doctrine about the *kategoriale Anschauung*, and, of course, the theses about both the predicative *being* and the *existence* –, this first

11. Miguel García-Baró

burst of Phenomenology suffers, as a whole, entirely from *naturalization of consciousness*, though not from *naturalization of ideas* (thanks to the implicit theological help coming from Brentano, much reinforced by the Bolzanian *Wissenschaftslehre* and the discussion of texts of Logic and Philosophy of Mathematics, especially Frege's, that Husserl so sternly carried out in the 1890s).

The *Logische Untersuchungen* would then represent a failed strike of genius, which is also very apparent in the mereological doctrine on the internal consciousness of time. This extraordinary strike of genius must have necessarily prevented its author against any philosophy *als Weltanschauung* and, when understood in depth, leads with perfect coherence into a quasi-idealistic, quasi-Kantian, phase in the development of the ultimate ontological framework of Phenomenology.

I have recently come to give more value to what I would now call *reism* of the later Husserl, starting from the understanding of the impossibility of the *Vernichtung der Welt* and a parallel further exploration of the teleological motives of Phenomenology. My doctoral thesis already rebelled against the transformation of the *Unzeitlichkeit des Idealen* in mere *Allzeitlichkeit*. For a moment, I thought myself closer to *Phenomenological realism* than I really was. This *"reism"* that I can now see in the later Husserl (and which I very succinctly present in a divulgation book about his thought that will soon appear in Spain) would allow us to overcome this paradox and others that hinder the phase of phenomenology when it was understood as *transzendentaler Idealismus*. And it is very interesting for a Spanish person to see how our own tradition had always anticipated this final turn in a way – so much so that Ortega could not admit it when he read the originally published fragment of *Krisis*. In his final phase, Xavier Zubiri – though through methods I cannot quite accept – has started out in this way of thinking, hardly ever followed by any of the *"realist phenomenology"* styles which arose after Husserl (the exception being, perhaps, its intimation in the works of Adolf Reinach and Edith Stein and also – though in a way that is too infused of Heidegger for me – in those of Jan Patočka).

But my personal investigations have also explored another field, in which I am currently more invested than in any other, and which I have been exploring in my books for the last 10 years, inspired both by Plato and my studies on phenomenology of religion (I must mention my teacher in this field, Juan Martin Velasco) and Theology, and even by my unpublished production in the field of poetry. I started out in it by noting how the question of evil, and especially that of moral evil, was not sufficiently dealt with in Husserl's works. From there I moved towards the general problem of freedom and, in this way, to the *transcendental genesis* of phenomenological reduction itself (a problem which Husserl, in spite of his efforts in, for instance, the *Sechste Cartesianische Meditation*, had left open). The concurrent study and Spanish translation of Franz Rosenzweig, Emmanuel Levinas and Søren Kierkegaard, and a redoubled interest for the *Shoah* and the literature about it, put me in the perspective of a narrative phenomenology of existence where not only freedom but also *occurrences* play decisive roles. From the general scheme of Rosenzweig (creation – revelation – redemption) I have seen a much more complex structure arise: death – guilt – love – tragedy – forgiveness, which continues to get richer and more nuanced. This enhancement is due, to a very important degree, also to the Platonism that I partly embrace, which makes me stand in anthropological matters in the proximity of the philosophy influenced by Vladímir Solov'ëv.

For all these reasons I have become an ever more radical critic of Martin Heidegger, at the same time as I moved closer to other directions within French phenomenology (Michel Henry and the current authors De Gramont, Falque, and especially Lacoste). I also continue my work in translation in this direction. I consider that a mutual fecundation between Phenomenology and Theology, such as that which drives the Castelli Coloquia, for instance, is of great importance.

3. What is the proper role of phenomenology in relation to other disciplines?

As far as formal sciences and theoretical natural sciences are concerned, the role of phenomenology is to just set limits to those abusive – and ultimately absurd – interpretations which want to see them as more than peculiar regional ontologies. Phenomenology especially needs to avoid the illusion that these sciences can invade the realm of first philosophy. In fact, it should continue to strive for an authentic regional phenomenological ontology of the *physis*. This field has not been worked on for a long time, to the resulting harm not only of philosophy, but also of culture in general.

As far as human and social sciences are concerned, the situation with respect to psychology is globally the same which Husserl diagnosed, although advances have been made about what is called deep psychology, developmental psychology and the theory of emotions. Phenomenological doctrines have interesting therapeutic applications, and the therapeutic practices sharpen the phenomenologist's vision about questions of great importance, such as the emotion of guilt, aggressiveness or, especially, what is known as resilience. There have been progress and mutual benefits also in sociology and anthropology.

Although phenomenologists obviously have a lot to learn from these disciplines, phenomenology is still not recognized in the role that corresponds to it *de iure*, as their epistemological and ontological foundation. Regional ontologies in these areas are impossible unless we resort to phenomenology in the radical sense that it has for Husserl, Levinas or Henry (although it is well known that these latter ones really speak of an *inversion* of it). In fact, no one has yet tried to establish a link between the very particular Levinasian "hermeneutics" – using *Totalité et infini* as a necessary starting point – and the need to restart works on a well-organized hierarchy of regional ontologies.

Phenomenology of religion deserves a separate chapter, because a fecund influence has flown from it to certain areas of phenomenology (as a fundamental philosophical science). I will mention three, which have arisen in Martín Velasco and the interaction between my own works and his: firstly, the notion of *Lebenswelt* is much enriched when we observe that the difference *sacred – profane* is that of two different ways to live everything, separated by a *passage ritual*. Secondly, the sphere of emotional states broadens with an important series of them that only the *homo religiosus* lives. Thirdly, a possibility of describing subjective life as endowed, although in different senses, with two *ego poles* rather than just one (the subjective personal and the divine one) may be afforded from a phenomenology of *liturgy* and, more concretely, of *prayer*.

Finally, we should progress in the appreciation by phenomenology of the most interesting and complex of all humanistic disciplines: philology. The analyses of worlds-of-life or even the common world-of-life are not possible except by paying the closest attention to the plurality of resources and history of the natural languages, even if with every methodological reserve which phenomenology must observe when facing this pending task.

4. What have been the most significant advances in phenomenology?

We should admit that nothing was more important to Husserl himself all along his life than to avoid the *naturalization* of either consciousness or the ideal in his works. In Husserl's personal trajectory phenomenology took more steps than it has ever since, in the near eight decades that have passed since his demise.

A notable problem of post-Husserlian phenomenology is its constant relapsing into nominalism. Also the ambiguity that reigns in respect to the limits of Life as submitted to the ontological horizon of the World.

To return to the achievements of Husserl himself, his *de facto* abandoning of the very idea of a formal ontology was incalculably important. Formal ontology ultimately prevents us from either treating Life adequately or paying a close attention to its non-living correlates – the peculiar dynamicity of the diverse noematic regions.

Heidegger is primordially credited with the introduction in Phenomenology of a bundle of Kierkegaardian, Augustinian and Pascalian motives (the various ways of temporalizing especially, which open new perspectives over the natural motivation of the authentic fulfillment of existence). On the other hand, our overall balance of Heidegger should not fail to consider some results of his work that are most disappointing. Two of them at least must be emphasized, which prevented him from linking phenomenology to ethics: his unfortunate conception of *Gewissen* and his historicist and relativist strain, which, in spite of the many subsequent attempts to the contrary, is still understood as a transformation of phenomenology into hermeneutics. Phenomenology is based on the utopia of perfect Good and freedom, on the teleology of reason (the practical one included, of course). But these matters fall too far from Heidegger's reach before and after the *Kehre*, and turn a very considerable part of the so-called Hermeneutics in a mere variation over themes that are Nietzschean at best, and otherwise anti-political, to put it mildly. Husserl was right to call Heidegger his *antipode*.

We can't but deeply lament that in Husserl's own work the question of freedom was left in the background. The influence of existential analytics and of the doctrine of *Seyn* and its fates limit, in a nominalist way, and hinder the original ethical impulse of thinkers so interesting as Merleau-Ponty and Patočka. (Something similar happened in Spain: the ethical-existential throb behind the best of Unamuno's works is weakened in Ortega, whose personal progression offers a parallel to the official history of the phenomenological movement: from phenomenology into hermeneutics.)

This is why I consider the works of Michel Henry and Emmanuel Levinas the most valuable, surpassed only by the voluminous exemplary work done by Husserl, because it was them who did the most for the progress of Phenomenology by criticizing Heidegger and the philosophical derivations that flow from him – whose Spanish parallel is Xabier Zubiri, even though his essays on the critique of estimative and practical reasons suffer from many insufficiencies or, to be fair, may have only been broadly drafted.

The misfortune at the basis of the historical origin of Brentano's school consisted in their being unacquainted with Maine de Biran. Henry has succeeded – more profoundly, by the way, that Funke – at making up for this hindrance, that for so long delayed the appropriate understanding between *chair* and *esprit*. Henry has shown the way to great possibilities in the description of affective life, more radically than Max Scheler, and has reinstated, very opportunely and with great merit, the prevalence of the *principle of all principles* against hermeneutics. Thanks to Henry, the splendid descriptive successes of French philosophy from Biran to Blondel, Bergson and Nabert, are open now to their integration and re-elaboration into phenomenology. Nevertheless, nominalism still hinders *material phenomenology* with an ample series of paradoxes.

The extreme notion of *alterity* to which Levinas has devoted all his life as a thinker represents the other great advance in phenomenology. It is interesting to note the virtually absolute tension that exists between Henry's philosophy of immanence and Levinas' philosophy of transcendence (which is less nominalistic, as it had to). Both of them are missing a real phenomenology of the *physis*, although it is clear that Levinas is more fertile in this direction. Emmanuel Falque, using the results – also, rather preliminary – of Merleau-Ponty as a starting point, will probably be able to contribute to this endeavor. And it is to this endeavor, I assume, where Zubiri's doctrine of the *dynamic structure of reality* could prove the most useful if known outside the Spanish-speaking environment.

5. What are the most important open problems in phenomenology and what are the prospects for progress?

The question of being is not the primordial one in philosophy. The "ontical" preeminence belongs to the double question of perfect good and truth. These are ultimately two sides of the same coin, of the same problem where everything, in human existence and nature, is at stake. Husserl went further than any other philosopher when exploring the realm of truth, but was less successful in the (detailed) exploration of the realm of good.

The problem that links these two realms is precisely that of *inter-subjectivity*, this is to say, the relation *self – other* (that being understood under the many ways it can be declinated, and still not letting aside the peculiar divine *interior intimo meo*, which I like to put as *this self who is more me than myself*). In this relation also the *Gesinnungen* and the actions on which good or bad achievement of existence fully depend (love, fear, violence, forgiveness, hatred, repentance, sin, atonement) are at stake. And on these radical spiritual options are later based the diverse *temporizations* of existence (despair, anxiety, peace, finiteness, beginnings of eternity, joy and suffering) and their astonishing *fruitfulness* (of spiritual, generative, educational, political, and artistic kind).

If I am convinced that nothing more than a very interesting bundle of partial approximations to truth has been attained in this whole realm which constitutes the cornerstone of the two decisive related problems, I am pointing out the hindrances of phenomenology itself, but only as it has been worked out until today. Perhaps philosophy itself, against Hegel's assumption, is only in its childhood...

The difficulties put forward to Phenomenology by the study of the relation between *self* and *other* by no means shall lead to a dead-end road; on the contrary, a further attempt to think more deeply those questions that the considering of intersubjectivity may arise, should mean an exciting challenge, as shown by the most relevant and apparent of them, mentioned above. The idea of philosophy (as an attempt at absolute responsibility towards the truths based on which one lives one's life) and the idea of its method ("*intuition*") that Husserlian phenomenology proposes are, as I receive them, perfect, if I am allowed the expression. When one enters the realm of narrative existential phenomenology, the *a posteriori* prevails over the *a priori* (because this is the realm of freedom, of the contingent, the gift and the surprise, in other words, it is precisely the inter-personal and what puts man in relation to the non-human beings in a sense beyond the cognitive; as Kierkegaard (or, rather, Vigilius Haufniensis) humorously said, second philosophy ends up being more true and important than first philosophy. But even this philosophy remains *second* phenomenology. (And the rest is not just silence but art, theology, fiesta, pain, hell and heaven.)

12

Sara Heinämaa

Academy Professor, Professor of Philosophy
Academy of Finland & University of Jyväskylä

---

1. Why were you initially drawn to phenomenology?
I started my path in phenomenology with Merleau-Ponty's *Phenomenology of Perception* as my sole guide and companion. I did not choose a solitary journey voluntarily but due to circumstances proceeded without teachers. I conducted my undergraduate and graduate studies at the Department of Philosophy in Helsinki in the 1980s, and this department was specialized in and devoted to analytical philosophy of language, formal semantics and Wittgenstein studies. No living flesh and blood phenomenologists were present, and even history of philosophy was considered merely an auxiliary or secondary topic. Most staff members did not know phenomenological classics or contemporary phenomenology, and several dismissed this philosophy outright as a confused form of psychology or else as an outdated Platonism.

Fortunately, the university libraries in Helsinki were excellent at that time, and due to the more pluralistic past of the discipline, provided the primary and secondary sources necessary for the outset of phenomenological investigations. This allowed me to proceed, in the guidance of the references that I found in the footnotes of Merleau-Ponty's *Phenomenology*, to study Husserl's *Ideas*, *Cartesian Meditations* and *Experience and Judgment*, and related sources. I was also lucky to have three teachers who, operating at the margins of departmental philosophy, gave course on Descartes, Hume, Peirce and Sartre.

But before philosophy – Wittgensteinian or Husserlian, analytical or continental – I explored four subjects that I learned to love in the high school: literature, art history, architecture and mathematics. I studied Gogol, Dostoyevsky and Kafka and learned to think about possibilities and necessities by reading *The Nose*, *Crime and Punishment* and Kafka's *America* or *The Missing Person* and by examining the drawings of Miró, Kandinsky and Escher. I also acquired some preliminary strategic skills and defense techniques by playing bandy and basketball. So without realizing it, I prepared for future life in philosophy.

I entered academic philosophy by plunging into analytical debates on the nature of science, language and mind at the Department of Theoretical Philosophy in Helsinki. The topic of my MA (1988) and licentiate theses[1] (1992) was the idea of *language of thought*, then dominant in philosophy of cognition. The idea was most vigorously propagated by Jerry Fodor and Noam Chomsky and their colleagues at MIT, but it was also developed in less austere forms by philosophers of mind, psychologists, linguistics and cognitive scientists.

In these two theses, I devised a Wittgensteinian critique of the idea of language of thought and for this end studied diverse sources, historical and contemporary, such as Sellars, Dummett, Putnam, Peirce, Saussure and Turing. The argument worked against causal theories of meaning and against internalist, representational and computationalist theories of thinking, but it also questioned the then ruling idea that all thought is compositional in structure and thus similar to language.

Here I was influenced by readings in the history of philosophy. The most important sources of inspirations and concepts were probably Descartes' *Meditations* and his *Passions of the Soul* that I studied under the guidance of my supervisor Professor Lilli Alanen. Professor Alanen challenged many received views and outworn conceptions of Descartes' philosophy and highlighted the epistemological and experiential aspects of his discussion of the mind-body union and human passions.[2]

I was intrigued, especially, by Descartes' paradoxical treatment of sensations and emotions. On the one hand, Descartes dismisses all passions as confused forms of thinking but, on the other hand, he also points out that their confusions are not essential but are grounded in our mental habits. This was a fresh notion in the philosophical environment of the late 20th century, and it suggested that we could grasp our sensory experiences distinctly even if they lack the propositional structures of judgments and thus cannot serve as grounds for inferences. Later, I wrote research articles on Descartes' theory of passions, most importantly on the emotion of wonder, and the relevance of this theory to contemporary phenomenology of embodiment and emotions. Professor Alanen's open-minded and pluralistic attitude in philosophy served as a model and as a source of inspiration.[3]

---

[1] In the Northern European academic system, the licentiate thesis is a pre-doctoral work that requires at least two years of independent research.

[2] For example, see Lilli Alanen's *Descartes's Concept of Mind* (Cambridge: Cambridge University Press, 2003).

[3] Lilli Alanen was student of two Finnish philosophers, Professors Georg Henrik von Wright and Erik Stenius who both propagated a pluralistic and equalitarian attitude in philosophical work. For this background, see Alanen 1997, 2014, cf. von Wright 1951, Stenius 1960, von Wright 1963a, 1963b, 1998,

Another important source of concepts and methods was Peirce's semiotics and his "phenomenology" or "phanerology" that I learned to understand thanks to the insightful seminars of my other supervisor Professor Leila Haaparanta. What proved useful in criticizing computational theories of cognition and thinking were Peirce's analyses of signs and signification. I found powerful concepts that helped me defend and develop my conviction that not all important signs are linguistic signs and not all thinking is linguistically signifying.

Thus, diverse readings in history of philosophy supported my project of questioning the validity of the idea of a language of thought. But I soon realized that the problems lie deeper than in limited concepts of thinking and signifying. The linguisticist paradigm was not just dominant in analytical philosophy of mind; it was also implicated by the Heideggerian principles that guided the argumentation of many continental philosophers, most importantly Derrida and Foucault. In this respect, Richard Rorty's *Philosophy and the Mirror of Nature* (1980) was an eye-opening read.

Merleau-Ponty's *Phenomenology* offered an alternative to the linguisticist paradigm. It provided two major arguments that helped me proceed from the impasses of philosophy of mind and opened new avenues for philosophizing, namely the argument for the primacy of perception, and the argument that perceptual and emotive experiences are founded on passive associative syntheses. I found Merleau-Ponty's approach both intriguing and highly convincing since it was attentive to the richness of human experiencing. But most deeply I was struck by the fact that his phenomenology tackled issues that had been neglected by philosophers for several centuries: motility, sleep, desire and sexuality.

This approach converged with my earlier interest in existentialism. In my first year at the university, I had received the Finnish translation of Simone de Beauvoir's *The Second Sex* as a Christmas present from my mother. At the same time I attended all the courses in existentialism that my university was able to offer. In one course we studied the first two parts of Sartre's *Being and Nothingness*, but did not discuss the last part that deals with embodiment and intersubjectivity. So it was only when I found Merleau-Ponty's *Phenomenology* some five years later, that I was able to make sense of Beauvoir's statement that "the body is not a thing but a situation (…) our grasp upon the world and the outline of our projects."[4]

One spring in the early 1990s my supervisor Professor Alanen invited a group of doctoral students to a scholarly dinner arranged by her col-

---

[4] Simone de Beauvoir, *The Second Sex*, trans. H.M. Parhsley (Harmondsworth: Penguin, [1949] 1987), 66.

leagues Professors Simo and Marja-Liisa Knuuttila. The Knuuttilas and their colleague Professor Juha Sihvola had the tradition of organizing vernal symposia and workshops with Professor Martha Nussbaum in Helsinki on various topics related to their common interest in history of philosophy and Aristotelian ethics.

At the dinner, Professor Nussbaum asked all the doctoral students about their research topics. I was somewhat shy at that time, and when my turn came I simply stated in a low voice that I studied Jerry Fodor's philosophy. My answer was full of frustration since I had already long struggled with a mixture of the concepts of representation, signification, causation, computation and meaning. Professor Nussbaum was not satisfied with my reply and inquired further if I had no other interests in philosophy. I hesitated for a while but then told her that I had a strong interest in the existentialist tradition and had studied, for some time already, Simone de Beauvoir's *The Second Sex* and its philosophical undercurrents. Professor Nussbaum asked: "Why not write your thesis about topics that interest you?" This suggestion gave me a completely new understanding of philosophy. I decided to abandon Fodorian theories of meaning and write my thesis on phenomenology of embodiment.

2. What are your main contributions to the field of phenomenology?

In philosophy at large, I am perhaps best known for the phenomenological account that I have developed of sexual difference. I have argued that the distinction between biological sex and social gender, dominant in human and social sciences but also in much of contemporary philosophy, does not serve the critical philosophical end of understanding how sexual difference is constituted and instituted in human experience. The sex/gender distinction draws – historically and systematically – from the traditional distinctions between mind and body, psyche and soma, and culture and nature, and repeats their philosophical problems.

Social-constructivist and historicist attempts to overcome these problems downplay and underestimate the material, corporeal and driven aspects of sexual identities and differences. But, more importantly, constructivist solutions do not problematize the nature-culture divide in a philosophically groundbreaking manner. Rather than questioning the divide as such they problematize the idea of the naturally given by extending the concepts of cultural production to cover also what is experienced as natural.[5] In the constructivist framework, nature is theorized as a social-historical construct or product, a very special kind

---

[5] It seems to me that the historical starting points of the Butlerian critique of the natural given are not merely in Foucault's Nietzschean genealogy or Marx's discussion of ideologies, but also in Sellar's critique of Kantian epistemologies and Rylean philosophy of mind.

of product to be sure – since it covers its own produced character – but a product all the same. Thus Judith Butler, for example, famously argues that gender "must also designate the very apparatus of production whereby the sexes themselves are established" (Butler 1990 7). This does not liberate us conceptually from the traditional nature-culture divide; it just draws the dividing line between the given and the made at a different point. I have argued that phenomenological tools are needed if we want to question this conceptual apparatus as a whole and clarify the experiential grounds and the limits of the ideas of sex and gender.

The phenomenological concept of meaning-constitution is a methodological concept and differs from the epistemological and ontological concepts of social-construction. In the phenomenological framework, both the sense of nature and the sense of culture are constitutive achievements, and both these senses turn out to be constituted in several different manners and orders. This allows us to understand how sexual difference can appear to us both as a natural phenomenon and as a social-cultural phenomenon, both personal and interpersonal, both given and constructed.

The task of phenomenologically accounting for the constitution of sexual difference is part of the larger undertaking of social phenomenology. My main contribution to this field is in my discussion of the different aspects of human embodiment and their implications for the phenomenological theory of intersubjectivity. This involves four related tasks: first, a phenomenological clarification of the different aspects of human personhood; second, an explication of the different attitudes in which we can study human beings and their bodies; third, an account of the constitution of the different meanings of bodies, such as thing, organism, bio-mechanism and expression; and fourth, working out the implications that these three accounts have for the phenomenolological theory of intersubjectivity and its constitutive functions.

Carrying out these tasks requires both systematic and exegetic work. I have written extensively on themes crucial to our understanding of corporeality, such as mortality, generativity, desire, pregnancy and old age. These reflections are based on fresh readings of Husserl's concepts of *Leib* and *Körper*, empathy, personhood and expression. I have also clarified Husserl's distinction between the personalistic attitude and the naturalistic attitude, and thereby shed light on the relations between psychic being and physical being and the divergent ways of investigating these ontic regions. Moreover, I have argued that Merleau-Ponty's distinction between anonymous perception and personal perception articulates a generative structure that is fundamental to human embodiment. Finally, I have studied the ethical and moral philosophical implications of our existence as finite bodily persons in interpersonal relations.

Much of this is still work in progress, but I hope to have demonstrated that "the problem of the sexes," as Husserl calls it in *The Crisis*, is not a marginal issue to phenomenology or to transcendental inquiries into sense-constitution. More fundamentally, I hope that my work serves to challenge the deep-seated preconception according to which embodiment and sensibility have no transcendental constitutive significance but belong among empirical or factual matters.

There is also one practical contribution that I would like to mention in this context. At the beginning of this century, I started to work systematically with two of my closest colleagues, Professors Dan Zahavi and Hans Ruin, to promote phenomenological research, scholarship and teaching in North Europe. In 2001, we established *The Nordic Society for Phenomenology* for this purpose. For more than fifteen years now, the society has served as an open forum for young philosophers interested in topics central to contemporary phenomenology and its history. The society has grown into a multinational institution with more than 800 members from across the world. I consider this to be a major contribution to philosophy at large since the field is still largely lacking in equalitarian and pluralistic platforms of discourse and our society provides a new standard for open exchange.

3. What is the proper role of phenomenology in relation to other disciplines?

For me, phenomenology is still a philosophical endeavor with transcendental and eidetic aims. This means that when we study experiences in a phenomenological fashion and with a phenomenological interest, then we aim at illuminating the necessary structural features and the possible variations of experiences as well as the conditions of such necessities and possibilities. Thus, phenomenology also casts light on the experiential grounds and the pre-experiential foundations of the positive sciences. This allows it to chart the limits of the sciences and to guard against various forms of dogmatism, be it psychologistic, historistic, logicistic, naturalistic, materialistic or idealistic.

These phenomenological tasks can be carried out only in close dialogue with the positive sciences. And it is not just one dialogue with this or that dominant science that we have to master; rather, a network of dialogues is needed as well as exchanges with both central and marginal sciences. Moreover, such dialogues must be constantly renewed since sciences are not fixed sets of convictions but dynamic and developing practices.

But dialogue is not fusion and exchange is not assimilation. That is to say, phenomenology does not have to abandon its transcendental and eidetic aspirations in order to cooperate with the other disciplines, to learn from them and about them and to assist them in their proper aims.

4. What have been the most significant advances in phenomenology?

I do not see phenomenology as an advancing science in a similar fashion to the positive sciences. Rather, I see it primarily as a methodological approach – transcendental and eidetic – that allows us to describe and understand ever new areas of experiencing. Phenomenology, as emphasized by its founders, is defined by its task-like character. It is a critical undertaking that investigates the fundamental aims and means of our practices, including the practices of theorizing, philosophizing and scientifically investigating what is the case.

At the same time, however, it is evident that during the last 15–20 years there have been significant new discoveries in phenomenological investigations of intersubjectivity, generativity, sociality, values and norms. Phenomenologists have advanced our philosophical understanding of the external, responsive and practical character of perception, of the power of social and moral emotions, such as shame, guilt and wonder, and of the experiential grounds of the normalizing institutions of health, gender and race. These new advances have demonstrated to the general philosophical audience that phenomenology is not just a powerful theory of cognition but provides new conceptual resources for the study of human communities and human persons.

5. What are the most important open problems in phenomenology and what are the prospects for progress?

For me the eidetic character of phenomenology is one of the pressing issues that should be discussed in more depth and width than so far. By this I mean clarification of the eidetic aims and methods of phenomenology and their relations to the other methodological aspects of the discipline, that is the transcendental and the genetic methods and the methods of dismantling (*Abbau*). One also needs to explicate how phenomenology as a discipline relates to the aims of mathematization and mathematical modeling. Concretely this involves questions that concern the phenomena of ideality: What do we mean when we speak of ideas and idealities in respect to experiencing, to the world and to the positive sciences? What if anything ultimately binds together the ideal structures of cognition, the mathematical ideas of number and the political idea of democracy? Further, this implies questions concerning fantasy and fiction and the structures of imaginative and signifying consciousness. Answering these questions involves explication of the operative concepts of idea and essence, but it also requires that we discuss the temporal and generative character of phenomenology and its ways of developing descriptive and analytical concepts.

The task of clarifying what Husserl meant when he spoke of phenomenology as an eidetic science is pertinent since it allows us to determine the limits of naturalization. In other words, I do not believe that clarification can be won in the debate on transcendental vs. naturalized phenomenology unless we explicate the eidetic character of phenomenology, and do so in the light of the new results provided by contemporary phenomenology, both systematic and exegetic.

13

Nam-In Lee

Professor of Philosophy
Seoul National University (South Korea)

---

1. Why were you initially drawn to phenomenology?
I was first exposed to phenomenology when I took a philosophy class as an undergraduate student at Seoul National University. In the spring of 1979, I took a course on epistemology taught by professor Jeon-Sook Hahn. In this course we read M. Merleau-Ponty's *The Primacy of Perception*, and in that work I was fascinated by the detailed phenomenological descriptions of the structure of perception. Thereafter I read Part 1 and Part 2 of E. Husserl's *Die Krisis der europäischen Wissenschaften und die transzendentale Phänomenologie*. Husserl's diagnosis of the contemporary human being as a being faced with a total crisis, his analysis of the structure of the crisis, and his proposal to overcome the crisis appealed to me. This is the reason I wrote my BA thesis on "The Structure of the Crisis in *Husserl's Crisis of the European Sciences and the Transcendental Phenomenology*" in 1980.

In 1981, I began my MA studies in philosophy and I examined Husserl's phenomenology intensively. I sought out courses that primarily dealt with Husserl's texts such as *Ideen zu einer reinen Phänomenologie und phänomenologischen Philosophie, Erfahrung und Urteil, Erste Philosophie, Phänomenologische Psychologie* etc. They helped me understand Husserl's phenomenology in a far more comprehensive manner than before. I also took a course dealing with Heidegger's interpretation of Hölderlin's poems. Moreover, I was able to form reading groups with peers who were also interested in phenomenology and we discussed Husserl's texts intensively. These reading groups contributed immensely to my understanding of Husserl's phenomenology. In 1983, I wrote my MA thesis on "The Idea and the Structure of the Sciences of Essences".

After I finished my MA thesis in 1983, I began my doctoral studies in philosophy at Seoul National University. At that time, South Korea was a developing country and so the university library was not equipped with enough primary and secondary literature on phenomenology.

Moreover, there was no chance for me to read Husserl's unpublished manuscripts in Korean. For this reason, I decided to go to Germany to finish my Ph.D. studies there. Fortunately, in 1986 I got a DAAD scholarship which allowed me to go to Germany and study with Professor Klaus Held in Wuppertal, who had been the assistant of Landgrebe at the University of Cologne, and who himself had been one of Husserl's assistants.

I have taken many courses in Wuppertal and Cologne. The most important one among them was The Phenomenological Colloquium held by Klaus Held, Antonio Aguirre and Heinrich Huni. The Colloquium took place every two weeks in the afternoon of Thursday. I attended the Colloquium from the fall semester of 1986 to the summer semester of 1991, when I finished my Ph.D. thesis. I would say that this Colloquium was of crucial importance in my intellectual development as a phenomenologist. The Colloquium made it possible for me to become a real phenomenologist.

When I went to Germany, I had three topics for my dissertation. One of them was "Edmund Husserl's Phenomenology of Instincts". In the fall of 1986, I visited the Husserl-Archive in Cologne and checked whether there were enough unpublished manuscripts that dealt with the problems of instinct. I realized that there were a lot of manuscripts on the issue of instinct and I was very excited to study them one by one. In the spring of 1991, I finished my dissertation on *Edmund Husserls Phänomenologie der Instinkte*, and got my Ph.D. in the summer of 1991. My dissertation was published in the Phaenomenologica series as *Edmund Husserls Phaenomenologie der Instinkte* (Dordrecht/Boston/London: Kluwer Academic Publishers, 1993). In August of 1991 I returned to Seoul, and from 1991-1995, I taught at various universities in Seoul as a part-time lecturer. Since 1995, I have taught phenomenology at Seoul National University for 23 years.

2. What are your main contributions to the field of phenomenology?

My main contributions to the field of phenomenology consist in the following: 1) discovery of new aspects of Husserl's phenomenology, 2) the promotion of dialogue between Husserlian phenomenology and post-Husserlian phenomenology / other streams of contemporary philosophy (such as hermeneutics, philosophy of life, critical philosophy, and deconstructive philosophy), 3) applied phenomenology, 4) the promotion of dialogue between phenomenology and East Asian philosophy, 5) development of phenomenology of instinct.

First of all, from the very beginning, one of the main aims of my research in phenomenology has been to discover new aspects of Husserl's phenomenology. For example, the first book of mine mentioned above, on *Edmund Husserls Phänomenologie der Instinkte*, aims to discover a new aspect of Husserl's phenomenology by providing a systematic reconstruction of Husserl's phenomenology of instincts as a transcendental phenomenology, on the one hand, and a correlative reinterpretation of the entire system of Husserl's transcendental phenomenology on the other hand. Thereafter I published some articles that attempted to further discover new aspects of Husserl's phenomenology, such as "Edmund Husserl's Phenomenology of Mood" (in: Zahavi and Depraz (eds.), *Alterity and Facticity*, Dordrecht/Boston/London: Kluwer Academic Publishers, 1998), "Practical Intentionality and Transcendental Phenomenology as a Practical Philosophy" (in: *Husserl Studies* 17, 2000), "Static-Phenomenological and Genetic-Phenomenological Concept of Primordiality in Husserl's *Fifth Cartesian Meditation*" (in: *Husserl Studies* 18, 2002).

Second, as I was studying Husserl's phenomenology in Germany, I realized that there are many misunderstandings of Husserl's phenomenology. Husserl's phenomenology was usually portrayed as a radicalized form of Cartesian philosophy. However, this is only one aspect of Husserl's phenomenology that could be compared to a big mountain range comprised of many big mountains (an expression used by James Hart, when I met him in the United States in 1998). Husserl's phenomenology as a radicalized form of Cartesian philosophy can be seen as the first big mountain, behind which there are numerous other big mountains of phenomenology that go well beyond the scope of the first mountain. There are similarities between these new faces of phenomenology and the various kinds of post-Husserlian phenomenology / various streams of contemporary philosophy. For this reason, it is of enormous value for the future of phenomenology to promote a dialogue between Husserl's phenomenology and the various forms of post-Husserlian phenomenology/various streams of contemporary philosophy. After I came back to Korea in 1991, I began to carry out dialogues between Husserl's phenomenology and the various forms of post-Husserlian phenomenology / various streams of contemporary philosophy. In 2004, I published *Phenomenology and Hermeneutics* (in Korean) where I attempted to promote a dialogue between Husserl and Heidegger. (In 2005, I was awarded the Prize of the National Academy of Sciences of the Republic of Korea for this book). In 2013, I published *The Phenomenology of Perception in Husserl and Merleau-Ponty* (in Korean) where I attempted to promote a dialogue between Husserl and Merleau-Ponty. Besides these two volumes, I have published many articles that attempt to clarify the relationship between Husserl and post-Husserlian phenomenology/various streams of contemporary philosophy such as "Phenomenological Reflections on the Possibility of First Philosophy"

(*Husserl Studies* 26/2 (2010)), "Phenomenology of Language beyond the Deconstructive Philosophy of Language" (in: *Continental Philosophy Review* 42/4, 2010).

Third, since I began to study phenomenology around the beginning of the 1980s, I have been interested in applied phenomenology (below in section 3-5, I will clarify what applied phenomenology is). When I went to Germany in 1986, one of the topics I had in mind for my dissertation, and which was related to applied phenomenology, was "The Phenomenological Foundation of the Empirical Sciences". Until 2000, I did not have time to engage myself with applied phenomenology. After 2000, many colleagues in Korea in other disciplines than philosophy, urged me to engage myself with applied phenomenology. I have been invited to give talks on various topics of applied phenomenology at different circles and societies, and I have published some articles on applied phenomenology such as "Phenomenology and Qualitative Research Method" (in Korean, *Philosophy and Phenomenological Research* 24, 2005), "Phenomenological Sociology" (in Korean, *Philosophy and Phenomenological Research* 33, 2007), "Phenomenological Clarification of the Difference between Quantitative Research and Qualitative Research" (in Korean, *Philosophy and Phenomenological Research* 55, 2012). On the basis of these articles, in 2014, I published *Phenomenology and Qualitative Research* (in Korean).

Fourth, as a phenomenologist in East Asia, one of the aims of my study in phenomenology is to promote dialogue between phenomenology and East Asian thought such as Confucianism, Buddhism or Taoism. I have published some articles on this topic and I am now working on a project to carry out a phenomenological interpretation of East Asian thought.

Fifth, ever since I published *Edmund Husserls Phänomenologie der Instinkte* in 1993, instincts have been a research topic of interest. In this respect, it should be noted that, in the past 20 years, the concept of instinct has been discussed in respect to various disciplines such as evolutionary biology, evolutionary psychology, linguistics, ethics, aesthetics, and phenomenology. However, the meaning of instinct still remains unclarified in many respects. In order to overcome this situation, it is necessary to elucidate the genuine meaning of instinct so that the discussion of instinct in these disciplines can be carried out systematically. In this respect, I have published an article on "The phenomenological clarification of the concept of instinct through a criticism of Gehlen's theory of instinct-reduction" (in Korean). Moreover, there are different kinds of instincts and it is invaluable to carry out research on each of them. In this respect, I have recently published a book on *The Phenomenology of Aesthetic Instinct* (in Korean).

3-5. What is the proper role of phenomenology in relation to other disciplines? What have been the most significant advances in phenomenology? What are the most important open problems and what are the prospects for progress?

These are important questions to which different replies could be provided. I will try to give my answers to these questions by dealing with the topic of 'applied phenomenology and the future of phenomenology', a topic that is directly or indirectly related to the three questions.[1]

More than 110 years have passed since Husserl published his *Logische Untersuchungen* and we have witnessed the eruption of a vast array of different kinds of phenomenology all over the world. Even though we have witnessed the eruption of various kinds of phenomenology, there are still abundant possibilities to develop phenomenology in other various directions. Applied phenomenology is one direction that future phenomenologists should pursue. In fact, there have been many attempts to develop applied phenomenology in various forms. In my view, however, applied phenomenology still has abundant possibilities to be developed in many different ways in relation to many different disciplines. As will be discussed below, applied phenomenology is a branch of phenomenology that has its origin in Husserl's *Ideas I*[2].

A) The concept of applied phenomenology in Ideas I

It is in section 62 of *Ideas I* that Husserl talks about applied phenomenology. As the title of section 62 "Epistemological Anticipation. The 'Dogmatic' and the Phenomenological Attitude" shows, Husserl deals with the distinction between dogmatic and critical science indicating "the epistemological antithesis between dogmatism and criticism" (*Ideas I*, 141). According to this distinction, critical science means phenomenology as "the science having the unique function of effecting the criticism of all others and, at the same time, of itself", whereas dogmatic science includes all "the sciences which require 'criticism' – and indeed, a criticism, which they themselves are essentially incapable of effecting"(*Ideas I*, 141).

What is important in this respect is the fact that, as a critical science,

---

[1] A detailed discussion of the issue of applied phenomenology will be published in a volume of the journal of the group of SEFE (Sociedad Española de Fenomenología).

[2] E. Husserl, *Ideen zu einer reinen Phänomenologie and phänomenologischen Philosophie. Erstes Buch: Allgemeine Einführung in die reine Phänomenologie*, Martinus Nijhoff: Den Haag, 1976; E. Husserl, *Ideas Pertaining to a Pure Phenomenology and to a Phenomenological Philosophy. First Book: General Introduction to a Pure Phenomenology*, trans. F. Kersten (The Hague: Martinus Nijhoff, 1982).

phenomenology is functionally related to all the possible sciences. Moreover, if all the dogmatic sciences could be reborn as genuine sciences through phenomenological criticism, phenomenology would be the science that includes all such genuine sciences. It is in this context that Husserl claims that "[i]t is the distinctive peculiarity of phenomenology to embrace within the sphere of its eidetic universality all cognitions and sciences and, more particularly, with respect to everything in them which is an object of immediate insight, or at least would have to be such if they were genuine cognitions." (*Ideas I*, 142).

According to Husserl, it is precisely this critical function of phenomenology that makes it possible to develop applied phenomenology. Thus, after dealing with the distinction between dogmatic science and critical science, he addresses the issue of applied phenomenology as follows:

> "The sense and legitimacy of all possible immediate starting-points and of all immediate steps in any possible method lie within its sphere of jurisdiction. Thus phenomenology includes all the eidetic (therefore unconditionally and universally valid) cognitions with which the radical problems of 'possibility' relating to any alleged cognitions and sciences become solved. As applied phenomenology, of essential necessity, it produces the ultimately evaluative criticism of each specifically peculiar science; and thus in particular, it determines the ultimate sense of the 'being' of its objects and the fundamental clarification of its methods." (*Ideas I*, 142).

It should be noted that the phenomenology discussed by Husserl in this passage is the transcendental phenomenology as the central topic of *Ideas I*. Thus, it is claimed implicitly that applied phenomenology is a kind of transcendental phenomenology. More specifically, it is a transcendental phenomenology that "produces the ultimately evaluative criticism of each specifically peculiar science", that is, each individual science. Husserl numbers two particular tasks of applied phenomenology: (1) the determination of the "being" of the objects of the individual sciences and (2) the ultimate clarification of their method.

What is applied phenomenology in *Ideas I*, and more specifically, what is it as a kind of transcendental phenomenology? In order to understand what it is, we have to pay attention to the fact that there could be two kinds of transcendental phenomenology, that is, a) transcendental phenomenology as a general transcendental phenomenology that attempts to clarify the general transcendental structures, on the one hand, and b) a specific transcendental phenomenology that attempts to clarify the specific transcendental structures that are valid only for a certain region of objects and in this way "produces the ultimately evaluative criticism of each specifically peculiar science", on the other hand. As the passage cited above shows, applied phenomenology in *Ideas I* is identical with the specific transcendental phenomenology related to a certain region of objects, not with general transcendental phenomenology.

In my view, however, the concept of applied phenomenology in *Ideas I* is too narrowly grasped and underdeveloped, as will be discussed below. I will now sketch out the concept of applied phenomenology.

B) Phenomenology as a universal science[3]

Since it is within the whole context of phenomenology as a universal science that applied phenomenology has meaning, prior to clarifying the concept of applied phenomenology, I will first introduce and explain the idea of phenomenology as a universal science.

Husserl conceives of phenomenology as an organic whole that comprises not only the various dimensions of philosophical phenomenology, such as transcendental phenomenology, formal ontology, and regional ontology, but also the empirical sciences that are grounded in philosophical phenomenology in one way or another. All of these various dimensions of phenomenology come together in phenomenology as a universal science, as adumbrated in the passage cited above: "Thus phenomenology includes all the eidetic (therefore unconditionally and universally valid) cognitions with which the radical problems of 'possibility' relating to any alleged cognitions and sciences become solved." As a universal science, then, phenomenology should embrace all the following dimensions of science.

The first dimension of phenomenology as a universal science embraces all the empirical sciences such as physics, chemistry, biology, sociology, history, economics, politics, anthropology, psychology, etc. These sciences deal with empirical facts and attempt to disclose their various aspects. For this reason, Husserl calls them the "sciences of matters of fact" *("Tatsachenwissenschaften")* (*Ideas I*, 15). Husserl calls the empirical science founded on philosophical phenomenology "the empirical phenomenology" (Hua XXXV, 483).

---

[3] I have dealt with this issue in more detail in: Nam-In Lee, *Phenomenology and Hermeneutics* (in Korean), Seoul: SNU Press, 2004, 32 ff.

The second dimension of phenomenology as a universal science is regional ontology. Regional ontology is the eidetic science that deals with the essential structure of regions of objects. A typical example of regional ontology is geometry that deals with space as the essence of extended objects. There are various other examples of regional ontology, including the pure theory of time, the pure theory of movement, phenomenological psychology as pure psychology, etc.

The third dimension of phenomenology as a universal science is formal ontology. Formal ontology deals with the formal essences of the objects in general. Typical examples of formal ontology are traditional formal logic, pure grammar, arithmetic, mereology, etc.

The fourth dimension of phenomenology as a universal science is transcendental phenomenology. It is the task of transcendental phenomenology to disclose the conditions of the possibility for the constitution of any object whatsoever. Constitution in this context means the way in which we experience any kind of objects. We can do transcendental phenomenological research not only with respect to the objects of the empirical sciences, but also with respect to those of regional ontology and formal ontology, since they are all the results of constitution.

C) Various dimensions of applied phenomenology – developed from the example of phenomenological sociology[4]

The idea of phenomenology as an organic whole enables us to sketch out the various dimensions of applied phenomenology. I will try to sketch out the various dimensions of applied phenomenology with the example of phenomenological sociology.

A phenomenological sociology as an applied phenomenology can be developed in a number of different ways corresponding to the various dimensions of phenomenology as a universally valid science (namely, the dimension of transcendental phenomenology, that of regional ontology, and that of the empirical sciences), since sociological facts can be investigated in terms of each of these three different dimensions. However, we cannot develop a phenomenological sociology in the dimension of formal ontology, since formal ontology is a formal science that is empty of contents. Correspondingly, we have to distinguish between three different dimensions of phenomenological sociology: the dimension of transcendental phenomenological sociology, that of ontological phenomenological sociology, and that of empirical phenomenological sociology.

---

[4] I have dealt with this issue in more detail in: Nam-In Lee, *Phenomenology and Qualitative Research*(in Korean), Paju: Hangilsa, 2014, 355 ff.

Empirical phenomenological sociology is a kind of empirical science, and since the aim of empirical science in general is to describe and explain various kinds of empirical facts, it attempts to describe and explain sociological facts. There are many kinds of the empirical phenomenological sociology that deal with the different regions of the sociological facts.

Ontological phenomenological sociology is a kind of regional ontology, and since the aim of regional ontology in general is to clarify the essential structures of facts, it seeks to elucidate the essential structures of sociological facts. Each kind of empirical phenomenological sociologies discussed above has its own ontological sociological phenomenology so there are as many kinds of the ontological phenomenological sociology as there are kinds of the empirical phenomenological sociology.

Transcendental phenomenological sociology is a kind of transcendental phenomenology, and since the aim of transcendental phenomenology, in general, is to clarify the conditions of the possibility of anything, it attempts to explicate the conditions of the possibility for the constitution of sociological facts. There are many different kinds of the transcendental phenomenological sociology that could be developed with respect to many different kinds of the sociological facts.

D) Assessment of the concept of applied phenomenology in Ideas I

We are now in a position to assess the concept of applied phenomenology in *Ideas I*. As discussed above, the concept of applied phenomenology in *Ideas I* is too narrowly defined and still underdeveloped. We saw that it is a kind of transcendental phenomenology that "produces the ultimately evaluative criticism of each specifically peculiar science" and aims at a determination of the "being" of its objects and the clarification of its fundamental methods. We called it specific transcendental phenomenology and thereby contrasted it with general transcendental phenomenology.

However, the concept of applied phenomenology as specific transcendental phenomenology in *Ideas I* is too narrow a definition. If we reflect on the various dimensions of applied phenomenology discussed above, we realize that, in fact, the concept of applied phenomenology in *Ideas I* is indeed too narrow. In this respect, the following points should be noted.

a) The concept of applied phenomenology in *Ideas I* is too narrowly defined, since it does not include regional ontology as one of its components.

b) The concept of applied phenomenology in *Ideas I* is too narrowly defined, since it does not cover the various kinds of empirical phenomenology. It is true that, in section 62 of *Ideas I*, making a distinction between the dogmatic sciences and phenomenology, Husserl seems to conceive of his phenomenology as an organic whole that might comprise not only transcendental phenomenology but also regional and formal ontology and empirical phenomenology. In this context, it should be noted that he identifies dogmatic sciences with "the sciences that require 'criticism' – and indeed, a criticism, which they themselves are essentially incapable of effecting" (*Ideas I*, 141). However, when he describes the tasks of applied phenomenology, he does not mention that applied phenomenology could have empirical phenomenology as one of its parts. Needless to say, empirical phenomenology is an important part of applied phenomenology and, still again, there are abundant possibilities to develop empirical phenomenology in various directions within various disciplines.

Thus, the assessment of the concept of applied phenomenology in *Ideas I* enables us to understand applied phenomenology more properly. It includes three different dimensions of phenomenology, namely the dimension of specific transcendental phenomenology, that of regional ontology and that of empirical phenomenology.

E) Why do we need to develop applied phenomenology?

Applied phenomenology has its own inalienable value, since it could clarify the structure of the various regions of objects from a phenomenological perspective. This is one of the reasons why it has to be pursued. However, it is, first of all, with respect to the contemporary crisis of humanity that applied phenomenology has to be pursued.

In order to cope with the contemporary crisis of humanity, we have to first develop a pure phenomenology and, on the basis of it, various disciplines of applied phenomenology. It is nothing but these various disciplines of applied phenomenology that enable us to cope with various kinds of crisis in the many sectors of contemporary human life. This is the reason why the development of various kinds of applied phenomenology in many different dimensions and disciplines is so urgent.

There have been various attempts to develop applied phenomenology from the very beginning of the phenomenological movement. Husserl was mainly interested in developing pure phenomenology, since it is the foundation of applied phenomenology. Needless to say, he also sought to develop applied phenomenology, as can be witnessed in his attempts to advance phenomenological psychology. Many phenomenologists after Husserl also attempted to develop applied phenomenology in many disciplines. A typical example is A. Schutz who contributed immensely to phenomenological sociology. Nowadays, there are lots of scholars who are doing research in applied phenomenology in various fields such as sociology, psychology, anthropology, political science, economics, communicology, management, education, nursing, geography, archaeology, ecology, literature, music, fine arts, film, sports, etc.[5] Still, applied phenomenology has great potentials to unfold itself further in new dimensions and disciplines. I think that one of the directions in which the phenomenological research of the 21st century should be headed more intensively is *applied phenomenology*.

---

[5] In his paper on "Interdisciplinarity within Phenomenology" that was presented at the 3rd PEACE Conceference in 2009 in Seoul, Lester Embree names more than 30 disciplines as follows: Archaeology, Architecture, Cognitive Science, Communicology, Counseling, Cultural Anthropology, Ecology, Economics, Education, Ethnic Studies, Ethnology, Ethnomethodology, Film Studies, Social Geography, Hermeneutics, History, Linguistics, Law, Literature, Medical Anthropology, Medicine, Musicology, Nursing, Philosophy of Religion, Political Science, Psychiatry, Psychology, Psychopathology, Religious Education, Social Work, Sociology, and Theology.

14

Dermot Moran

Professor of Philosophy
University College Dublin (Ireland)

---

1. Why were you initially drawn to phenomenology?
I first began to read philosophy (or at least philosophical novels) in Secondary School, while still deciding what course to study at university. It was probably 1968, a heady time, and I can remember buying Jean-Paul Sartre's *Nausea* and *The Age of Reason*, the first book of his trilogy of existentialist novels. Sartre's conception of radical freedom was intoxicating and in line with the mood of the times. Sartre was a great writer; he dramatized philosophical problems. Furthermore, Sartre was prominent in the news at that time as a philosopher leading the workers and students' revolutions of May 1968. He continued to be a very well known public intellectual through the Seventies with his controversial embrace of radical causes; for example, his well publicized visit to Andreas Baader of the Baader-Meinhof Group in Stammheim prison in 1974. Philosophy – especially Sartre's existentialism tinged with social commitment expressed in Marxist and Maoist terms –seemed very attractive and relevant to young people—it was of course utterly destroyed once news broke of the Khmer Rouge atrocities in Cambodia (Pol Pot was allegedly inspired by French Marxism).

My secondary school, Oatlands College, placed a strong emphasis on mathematics, physics, chemistry, and the sciences generally, and prepared students for university courses in engineering, medicine and science. I myself was debating between pure physics and chemistry but eventually enrolled in Mathematics at University College Dublin in 1970. It was in the days before computerized registration in the university and I was able to enroll officially in the BA in Mathematics and English – only to discover three weeks into the course that the lectures in Mathematics were scheduled at the same time as the lectures in English (seemingly, no one had ever proposed that degree combination before). I decided to opt for English and Philosophy as my major.

The Philosophy curriculum at UCD had been primarily Neo-Thomist but, due to student agitation in 1969 (the year before I arrived), the course had been broadened to include lectures on Marxism and Existentialism (including Sartre). Nevertheless, it was probably not until the final year of my BA undergraduate studies in 1973 that I encountered Phenomenology as such in a course with a very learned and scholarly priest, Rev. Dr. John Chisholm C.S.SP. He held two doctorates, had studied in Switzerland, and spoke German. Although by instinct a Thomist, he knew the works of Husserl and Heidegger at first hand and was a very careful and balanced exegete. I still own the copies of the English translations of Husserl's *Ideas*, Heidegger's *Being and Time*, Sartre's *Being and Nothingness*, and Merleau-Ponty's *Phenomenology of Perception*, that I bought for that course. The connection between Thomism and phenomenology was greatly helped by the fact that the Catholic University of Leuven, a renowned center for Neo-Thomism, was also host to the Husserl Archives, which had been set up by the Catholic priest Fr. Leo Herman Van Breda. Furthermore, for Thomists, Heidegger's interest in ontology was seen as offering a necessary corrective to the anti-metaphysical stance current in analytic philosophy of the time, e.g. A. J. Ayer's *Language, Truth and Logic* (1936), or Wittgenstein's *Philosophical Investigations*, which dismissed metaphysical questions as non-sense or as ill-formed.

As an undergraduate, I was particularly interested in Heidegger, because his basic question concerning the "meaning of Being" (*Sinn von Sein*) seemed – in the truly phenomenological manner—to cut transverse across the question of being as it had been discussed in traditional metaphysics and I was, of course, very familiar with the Neo-Thomist tradition of interpretation of Aristotle through Thomas Aquinas and modern commentators such as Étienne Gilson (e.g. his *Being and Some Philosophers*, 1949) or Joseph Owens' *The Doctrine of Being in the Aristotelian Metaphysics* (1963). For instance, Jacques Maritain argued that all knowledge, and indeed all conscious awareness, had to be based on a prior *intuition* of being, whereas other Thomists based the apprehension of being on the positing involved in the act of judgment. These debates fascinated me and, of course, gave a detailed context to the analysis of Being given by Heidegger or the discussion of categorial intuition in Husserl's Sixth Logical Investigation. Heidegger's claim that ontology can only be pursued through phenomenology led me to read phenomenology in greater depth.

Moreover, Heidegger's insistence in *Being and Time* that the everyday existential structures of human being, Dasein, had to be understood before the question of the meaning of Being in general could be raised intelligibly, struck me as revolutionary. It was, of course, a Kantian, critical move and hence Heidegger interpreted his phenomenology as *transcendental* philosophy, something I have continued to insist upon

(Moran 2007a). But it was now easy to see how Heidegger's claim that the essence of Dasein lies in its existence could be taken up as the basis of Sartre's existentialism. Human existence is never complete but is lived through historically. This insight seems still to be missing from analytic philosophy.

My PhD studies at Yale (beginning in 1973) also focused on Heidegger, directed by my doctoral supervisor Professor Karsten Harries (one of the few philosophers invited to contribute to Heidegger's eightieth-birthday Festschrift, published by Niemeyer in 1970). Heidegger's death in May 1976 coincided with my "admission to candidacy" at Yale – where one is supposed to propose and defend one's dissertation topic in detail in front of one's supervisory committee. I had been planning to re-examine critically Heidegger's accusation that the Medieval Scholastics had focused on substance and showed "forgetfulness of being" (*Seinsvergessenheit*). Heidegger's *Frühe Schriften* (1972) had only recently been published by Klostermann, which included his Habilitation thesis: *Die Kategorien- und Bedeutungslehre des Duns Scotus* (1916), so it was now possible to study Heidegger's Neo-Scholastic origins at first hand. Harries had made me aware of Heidegger's interest in Meister Eckhart (to whom Heidegger had promised to dedicate a book). However, I decided in the end to focus for my dissertation on someone who influenced Eckhart, namely, the Irish medieval Neoplatonist John Scottus Eriugena, because his complex and subtle account of being and non-being (and his fourfold division of nature) seemed to directly challenge Heidegger's negative assessment of the medieval in relation to the meaning of Being. Indeed, Eriugena's analyses of the various meanings of non-being in his *Periphyseon* seemed quite close in spirit to Heidegger's musings on the relation between being and non-being in his 1929 inaugural lecture at Freiburg, *What is Metaphysics?*, and refuted Heidegger's claim that the Medievals did not fully grasp the question of the meaning of Being.

So I wrote my dissertation on the philosophy of nature of John Scottus Eriugena (Moran 1987), and its relation to idealism, published as *The Philosophy of John Scottus Eriugena. A Study of Idealism in the Middle Ages* (Moran 1989) but I always was thinking of these medieval disputes in relation to phenomenology and especially Heidegger. So my interest in medieval philosophy was always driven by a phenomenological horizon (Moran 2014a).

I have always been drawn towards idealism, whether it be in the form of Plotinian monism, Eriugenian meontology (Moran 1999), Berkeleyan immaterialism, Kantian critical philosophy, Hegelian absolute idealism or, latterly, Husserl's transcendental idealism (Moran 2006). Husserl's claim in *Ideas I* that consciousness in a certain sense has priority over being makes sense from the point of view of the mode of access to phenomena and a similar claim could also be found in the Neoplatonic tradition (from Plotinus to Eckhart and Dietrich von Freiburg). For me, then, there is a natural affinity between transcendental phenomenology and transcendental idealism and various forms of contemporary anti-realism (as found in Hilary Putnam, for instance, see Moran 2000c).

It was a long while before I moved back from Heidegger to reading Husserl very closely (by then I was lecturing in Belfast) and I did so primarily to understand how Heidegger's question of the meaning of being emerges from his reading of Brentano's *On the Several Senses of Being in Aristotle* and Husserl's discussion of categorial intuition in the Sixth Logical Investigation (as Heidegger himself claimed in his fascinating 1963 essay "My Way to Phenomenology", *Mein Weg in die Phänomenologie*). Reading Husserl's *Logical Investigations* in relation to Heidegger convinced me of the close affinity between their projects, especially as Heidegger's Marburg lectures began to be published, most notably his 1925 *Prolegomena zur Geschichte des Zeitbegriffs* (Gesamtausgabe volume 20 published in 1979). Here at last was the missing evidence that showed precisely how Heidegger radicalized reinterpreted Husserl's conception of intentionality as really expressing the transcendence of Dasein (see Moran 2014c; Moran 2015c).

I carried out a long study over several years of Husserl's *Logical Investigations* (Moran 2001) The overall problematic is to understand how the independent concepts, objects, and truths of the sciences (e.g. the Pythagorean Theorem) are constituted as independently valid and timelessly true, despite the fact that they emerge only in the contingent, intentional practices of temporally-bound human subjects. In the *Logical Investigations* Husserl only has a basic intuition about phenomenology but his later development in *Ideas* and *Cartesian Meditations* is consistent with his overall approach in the *Investigations*. In my monograph on Husserl (Moran 2005), therefore I emphasized the continuity in Husserl's thinking against those interpreters who sharply distinguish between his thought before and after 1907.

Husserlian phenomenology begins from the recognition that human awareness is intentional, directed beyond itself at 'objects' and 'states of affairs' that it both intends as meaningful and encounters as already meaningful. Right to the end of his career, e.g. *Crisis of European Sciences* § 68, Husserl continues to invoke the "universal problematic of intentionality" and the "problem entitled intentionality" (*der Problemtitel der Intentionalität, Crisis* § 20) as the underlying theme of his phenomenology. Husserl presents intentionality, furthermore, as a *problematic*, even a mystery, rather than as any kind of *explanation* or *theory* or *solution* to an epistemological problem. Intentionality is a *phenomenon* that typifies human being-in-the-world (Moran 2013a). It can be described. For Husserl, from the phenomenological perspective, intentionality and sense-constitution more or less summarize the whole programme of philosophical investigation. Heidegger does not depart from this view in *Being and Time*: he is interested in *sense (Sinn)* albeit that it is primarily the "meaning of being".

For Husserlian and Heideggerian phenomenology, all experience, all being, all meaning, is correlated with human intentional comportment (*Verhalten*) (Moran 2003). This is an extra-ordinary rich insight. Of course, it can be caricatured as "correlationism", as in the recent critique of Quentin Meillassoux, but phenomenology insists – and is right to insist – that things, events, social structures, "objectivities" (*Gegenständlichkeiten*) of all kinds, have the meaning or sense that they do due to the human intentional constitution (which itself is mediated through our bodily incarnation, enworldedness and intersubjective cooperation). The notion that all cultural entities and institutions are culturally constructed (as proposed by Foucault and others) has now become such a dogma in the social sciences (especially in relation to the social construction of gender and race) that it has become unquestionable and has undermined the possibility of a genuinely critical discourse about the modes of being of social entities and their layers of constitution. Phenomenological constitution is more complex and more powerful tool that social constructionism. Husserl, for instance, is absolutely insistent – against cultural relativists- - that scientific objects (e.g. Newton's laws of motion) are posited as universally binding. It is a feature of our intentional practice that certain objects are constituted as abiding and unchanging. Truth for Husserl (and Habermas follows him here) has an inbuilt claim to unconditionality. As he writes in the *Logical Investigations* (Hua XVIII 134), truth requires "the unrestricted validity for all times' (*die unbedingte Geltung für alle Zeit*). The underlying phenomenological structures of intentional constitution deserve an important place in philosophical reflection and analysis. Husserlian phenomenology really proposes that human beings are meaning-apprehenders and meaning bestowers in a world that is encountered as already laden with significances that humans both uncover and, in a certain sense, compose.

Already in the *Logical Investigations*, Husserl accuses Kant (and at least his then current generation of Neo-Kantians) of misunderstanding the subjective domain as if it were something natural or "real", and hence of construing the a priori as if it were an essential part of the human species (*Logical Investigations*, *Prol*. § 38). Husserl very brilliantly diagnosed the incoherence inherent in the project of the "naturalization of consciousness".

Phenomenology, for instance, is rightly critical of the modern representationalist tradition in philosophy that stems from Descartes and Locke. Instead of beginning with a concept of mental representation taking place 'inside the head', it is more useful to think of 'sense', 'meaning', or 'significance' (*Sinn, Bedeutung*) as emerging from human intersubjective interaction or comportment constituting a world of significance within which objects and subjects find their sense (and Hubert Dreyfus has captured this correctly even if he mistakenly caricatures Husserl as a Cartesian representationalist). Husserl speaks of 'sense-apprehension' (*Auffassung*) or 'sense-explication' (*Auslegung*), or even 'interpretation' (*Interpretation*), since, in many cases, including the primal case of perception --which for Husserl is always basic to our human being-in-the-world, something that troubled the more 'pragmatic' Heidegger-- the constituted, sense-contentful object simply *appears or manifests itself* in a meaningful manner to a seemingly passive perceiving subject. In this regard, Merleau-Ponty's account simply develops Husserlian insights (Moran 2010a; Moran 2015a).

Phenomenological constitution means that human beings load their experience with sense or meaning, although they are almost never explicitly conscious of so doing, especially when conducting life "in the natural attitude". Constitution is largely an activity that takes place in the background, apart from those instances where conscious decision-making takes place at the level of judgment. To constitute means broadly to load or invest with meaning but it is, as I have been stressing, more a matter of being in tune with a pre-established significance. The perceived object is *always already* constructed, constituted, packaged and pre-digested for human consumption, as it were, and in most cases the subject's position is simply one of acceptance. Constitution is not so much a matter of casting a net of meaning over a meaningless entity but as apprehending and perceiving the already established meaning but a meaning that has been constituted by lower-level passive syntheses including the elusive temporal syntheses that lie at the very bottom of the flow of consciousness.

The natural attitude, for Husserl, is a very *thick* attitude; it presents us with the ready-made world, and one of the great challenges of phenomenology is to contemplate this attitude and understand its workings (this is the function of the transcendental epoché). I regard the identification of the natural attitude as one of the great breakthrough discoveries of Husserlian phenomenology.

2. What are your main contributions to the field of phenomenology?

I have been publishing broadly on phenomenology since the 1980s writing primarily on certain figures (Brentano, Husserl, Heidegger, Sartre,

Edith Stein, Theodor Adorno (Moran 1985), Hans-Georg Gadamer) and on certain themes such as intentionality, embodiment (Moran 2011a; Moran 2015b), empathy (Moran 2004), historicity (Moran 2011; Moran 2016), the constitution of sociality and culture, as well as in the critique of naturalism in philosophy (Moran 2008). My *Introduction to Phenomenology* (Moran 2000) set a new standard for understanding and discussing the phenomenological movement and its contribution. In particular, I tried to explain phenomenological concepts (intentionality, essence, constitution) and insights (the finitude of human existence) in the language of contemporary philosophy and hence I have opened up phenomenology to be understood and discussed within the dominant analytic tradition of philosophy in particular (see also Moran 2010). For this reason, I began with the discussion of Brentano on intentionality (Moran 1996). Brentano, in many ways, is the father of both analytic and continental philosophy. His concept of exact philosophy influenced both the Vienna Circle and Edmund Husserl (Moran 2000a). Brentano's notion of intentionality had a significant formative influence on Husserl's method of phenomenological description (Moran 2007) but it also – through the work of Roderick Chisholm — had an enormous influence on Anglophone philosophy of mind, from Quine to Dennett, Searle and Fodor. Perhaps one of the most important contributions I have made is to show that intentionality is a topic that has been discussed by both analytic and continental philosophers as part of a long continuum (Moran 1996a; Moran 1999a). If one looks at the treatment of topics across traditions one finds much greater room for discussion and dialogue. The concepts of intuition and essence, for instance, also deserve to be explored across the current analytic/Continental divide. One point I have always insisted on is that concepts have history and it is part of philosophical exploration to limn the contours of concepts historically and synchronically (see Moran 2013a). We need to know what we mean when we speak of "intention ", "mind," "action," "motivation," and so on.

Besides writing an updated history of the phenomenological movement (complementing the groundbreaking work of Herbert Spiegelberg), I see myself as contributing to various contemporary debates concerning, e.g. the understanding of intentionality, embodiment and sociality, and also in seeking to show to the dominant and historically innocent analytic philosophy that many of its current preoccupations actually consist of the revival of issues originally discussed by phenomenology. In several essays, I have been particularly strong in emphasizing the continuity between Husserl, Heidegger and Merleau-Ponty, against those critics (e.g. Hubert L. Dreyfus and to a certain extent Richard Rorty) who want to contrast Husserl's Cartesianism with Heidegger's "coping" (see Moran 2010a).

Since I interpret phenomenology as inherently a transcendental philosophy, I have also been vocal in the debate over the limits of naturalism (Moran 2008; Moran 2013b). Husserl was prescient when he identified *naturalism* as the greatest threat to the possibility of both genuine science and of genuine philosophy. Indeed, he believed that naturalism was not just a philosophical error but even threatened the preservation of genuine human values and the possibility of living a fully rational, communal life. Heidegger is also resolutely a transcendental and thus anti-naturalistic philosopher. The issue of Merleau-Ponty is more complicated and indeed it is his approach that has inspired "naturalized phenomenology" such as it was found in Francisco Varela and others. In my view it is a mistake to think of naturalized phenomenology as a real possibility. It misses the *epoché* and the implied transcendental turn. Husserl and Heidegger (and, in my view Merleau-Ponty) have always insisted that naturalism essentially misconstrues and mischaracterizes the irreducibly *intentional* nature of consciousness. Naturalism (and 'objectivism') begins from the presumption of a given 'ready-made world' and is opposed to Husserl's transcendentalism (*Crisis* § 14).

In his *Cartesian Meditations* § 20, Husserl criticizes Brentano for failing to exploit to the true potential of intentional analysis, claiming that he remained imprisoned in "naturalistic prejudices" that prevented him from understanding the role of synthesis and constitution. Inherent in the natural attitude is a certain conception of reality, truth and validity. The natural attitude has its own forms of verification, reliability and confirmation. It is the default attitude, the 'always already' attitude, *die Geradehin-Einstellung*, as Husserl's student Eugen Fink calls it (Moran 2008). It cannot as such be completely unplugged, although it can be highlighted, foregrounded, thematized, through a special reflexive act of attention that Husserl first describes in print as the 'radical alteration' (*Ideas I* § 31) of the natural attitude. Naturalism (viewed from the transcendental standpoint) is the natural product of the 'natural attitude', construed as the 'naturalistic attitude'.

In the last decade, I have been one of the phenomenologists (along with Dan Zahavi) who have revived the discussion of empathy in relation to the experience of other selves, and to demonstrate the strength of phenomenological resources in this area. In this regard, I have paid particular attention to the original contribution of Edith Stein (Moran 2004). I am genuinely interested in promoting Edith Stein as a major, neglected thinker. In that respect, I have also become interested in another neglected woman phenomenologist Gerda Walther (1897-1977), who wrote on the phenomenology of mystical experience. Husserl's period in the University of Göttingen (1901-1916) was notable for the fact that he attracted a significant number of women philosophers, including Hedwig Conrad-Martius (1888-1966), Gerda Walther, Elfride Petri (1893-1992, who married to Heidegger in 1917) and Edith Stein (1891-1942). Stein followed Husserl to Freiburg and became his first salaried assistant (1916-1918). She assisted in the editing of his *Ideas II* manuscript as well as his time-consciousness lectures (later published, without alteration, by Heidegger in 1928). In one of her letters she indicates her departure from Husserl and her agreement with Hedwig Conrad-Martius (whom Husserl appears to have frozen out after she disagreed with him) that there was a real world independent of consciousness and that this real world was a necessary condition for consciousness. Stein defends realism (and later a Thomistic-informed ontology) in opposition to Husserl's idealism, although Husserl in fact always maintained that empirically consciousness depends on material substrate, i.e. embodiment. Husserl shows his own awareness of her position when he adds a note to his edition of *Ideas* I, § 46 p. 103 (Husserliana III/1 Schuhmann edition, Appendix 44) that it should be noted that the physical thing must exist for experience to continue harmoniously and adds 'Miss Stein believes this might become misunderstood').

Following several projects on consciousness and embodiment, I have been involved in intensive research in the phenomenology of embodiment. Embodiment is an issue that is currently challenging philosophy of mind and action as well as the cognitive sciences. In particular I have demonstrated that Merleau-Ponty's conception of flesh (*la chair*) and of the 'intertwining' (*l'interlacs*) are actually developments of Husserl's position on embodiment (*Leiblichkeit*) rather than departures from it (Moran 2014; Moran 2015a).

Phenomenology has contributed hugely to the understanding of social and historical constitution and I have been involved in a research project, *Discovering the "We"*, on the phenomenology of sociality (Moran 2016). In similar vein, analytic philosophy of history is a particularly depressed and moribund region of research in contrast to the immensely rich discussions of historicality found in Husserl, Dilthey, Heidegger, Gadamer and others. Of course, I include Gadamer as a hermeneutic phenomenologist deeply influenced by both Husserl and Heidegger as is clear from his *Truth and Method* (Moran 2011).

There is in analytical philosophy (despite the short-lived interest in the history of analytic philosophy) very little attention paid to the historicity of human existence. In fact, even Foucault, who has enormous influence in certain areas of social philosophy, has a much poorer understanding of the "apriori of history" than Husserl (from whom Foucault borrowed the term, see Moran 2016a). So currently I want to expand my studies in phenomenology beyond intentionality, embodiment, empathy and sociality to the experience of living in history, culture and tradition (hence my interest in Husserl's *Crisis*, Moran 2012; see also Moran 2013).

3. What is the proper role of phenomenology in relation to other disciplines?

Phenomenology is not and can never be the whole of philosophy nor is it, *contra* Husserl and Heidegger, the foundational discipline of philosophy. Nevertheless, it has not been bypassed by postmodernism or made redundant by contemporary analytic philosophy of mind. Phenomenology is particularly strong in current intercultural discourse especially in China, for instance. Phenomenology has made and can continue to make significant contributions to all disciplines in philosophy, from philosophy of mathematics, physics, science, to ontology, epistemology and philosophy of mind, and also, especially, as I have been emphasizing to the sciences of history and culture (an area also pursued by Neo-Kantians such as Ernst Cassirer).

Analytic philosophy has of course become the dominant mode of doing philosophy in the English-speaking world but it tends to be practiced (with a few notable exceptions) in complete disinterest to its historical and cultural context (the discussions of the metaphysics of theism and the divine attributes in analytic philosophy of religion are particularly good case in point of a kind of reification of the divine and an absolutization of a certain Christian "god of the philosophers").

The very ubiquity of Anglophone analytic philosophy has given it a certain myopia. It is felt that any topic can simply be broached without any reference to the preceding discussions in the area (John R. Searle's analyses of intentionality and the construction of social reality are exactly of this kind; he willfully ignores that Husserl, Schutz, and others have ploughed these fields in very similar vein). The analytic "attitude", as it were, operates with all kinds of concealed and unquestioned assumptions and presuppositions. Certain disciplines tend to be accorded canonical status, at one time it was linguistic analysis (which could magic away philosophical problems), then it was philosophy of mind, now, ironically, it is analytic metaphysics – which was a contradiction in terms for the Vienna Circle and Positivist tradition. Most recently, analytic philosophers have embraced themes that would have been traditionally associated with the Continental tradition (e.g. the social construction of gender and race). Phenomenology simply needs to become more vocally involved in contemporary debates. Phenomenology has actually made enormous contributions to analytic philosophy of mind in reminding those philosophers of the complexity of conscious experience. For instance, phenomenology emphasizes the unity of the temporal flow of consciousness, a topic that is rarely foregrounded in analytic discussions. Similarly, the way in which the ego or self inhabits the stream of consciousness is a fertile field for phenomenological analyses (overcoming various Lockean assumptions that still dominate analytic discussions).

4. What have been the most significant advances in phenomenology?

Phenomenology, in my opinion, has been the most influential movement of the twentieth century in European philosophy, in terms of the range of disciplines and topics it has addressed and the number of counter-movements it has inspired. Jacques Derrida's deconstruction is unintelligible if one does not follow his thought through is essays on Husserl, in particular. Even Theodor Adorno devoted several of his major books to the critical discussion of Husserl and Heidegger. Phenomenology managed to retain the focus on subjectivity after it has been disastrously banished from twentieth-century thought by a very crude behaviorism (found from Watson to Skinner and Quine). Phenomenology, as I have suggested above, has made enduring contributions on central current topics from the nature of perception, the intertwining of the senses, the experience of embodiment, the understanding of others (empathy) and the nature of intersubjective social and collective life. In these topics, analytic philosophy has been playing catch-up since the 1960s (think of Hilary Putnam's slogan that the mind and the world jointly make up the mind and the world, for instance, surely an articulation of a phenomenological and "correlationalist" insight, although Putnam labels it "Hegelian"). Similarly McDowell and Brandom have been reviving Neo-Kantian and Hegelian insights, but these insights receive a very powerful critical treatment in phenomenology also, and this should not be neglected.

5. What are the most important open problems in phenomenology and what are the prospects for progress?

I think it is important to recognize that phenomenology is not so much a method as a tradition of maintaining a certain *attitude* towards philosophical problems, involving, a certain suspension of explanatory hypotheses drawn from other sciences (the epoche), an alertness to significance and to the subjective component in the constitution of objectivities of various sorts. Various versions of the phenomenological method (involving bracketing, reduction to essence) have been integrated quite successfully into qualitative research methods as used in psychology and in the human sciences (often involving intensive interviews with relatively few participants rather than large quantitative surveys). Having the right attitude or right mode of access to the phenomena under interrogation is crucial. In this sense, the procedure of phenomenology is comparable with the practice of the later Wittgenstein of diagnosing the presupposition at the heart of the initial philosophical question. A lot of genuine philosophical insight can be obscured if one rushes as the philosophical "Police" (as I call them) rush to declare: "that's not a philosophical question" or even "the real philosophical issue here is …". It is important to attend to the phenomena.

The twentieth century has made some disastrous decisions in regards to the methodologies of science. Husserl, for instance, was correct to identify the turn to naturalism and also the embrace of positivism and behaviorism as extremely detrimental to the project of genuine science. Gradually late 20th-century philosophy of mind rediscovered the issues (intentionality, consciousness, embodiment, sociality) that had been central to phenomenology from the outset. When analytical philosophy of mind finally emerged from the stranglehold of behaviorism, which had inhibited it from the 1920s to the beginning of the 1960s, it had to struggle to show the value of the concept of intentionality and then consciousness, giving rise to the work of Searle, Dennett, and others. Phenomenology, especially in its analyses of non-linguistic perception, helped to defeat the widespread assumption of philosophy of language that *all* meaning was enshrined in linguistic behavior.

It seems to me that the most open question is still the issue of the constitution of meaning. Social constructivism too easily assumes that all meanings are products of contingent human behavior, with an underlying commitment to cultural relativism. Phenomenology's concept of meaning-constitution is much more complex and nuanced and is explicitly anti-relativist in orientation.

More recently philosophy of mind realized it had to forget about modeling minds on computers and recognize the inherent lived embodiment of human consciousness. More recently still the individualist approach in philosophy of mind has been challenged by the recognition of the inherently social and contextually embedded nature of lived conscious experience. There are many further resources that still remain untapped in the phenomenological tradition, including the experience of being, which will eventually attract the attention of analytic metaphysicians.

Phenomenology has, from the outset, most interesting insights into human temporality and historicity: what it is to live as a human being across time (from youth to old age), how one shares an outlook with one's family or economic class or generation, how one belongs to the evolving horizons of history. These are all significant questions which philosophy needs to address. Contemporary analytic philosophy has almost no understanding of the dynamics of history (aside from what is somewhat woodenly assumed among the few contemporary Hegelian and Marxist philosophers).

A giant open question in philosophy, which could be addressed usefully by phenomenology, is the question of what it means to be a person. The concept of the person -- under different designations-- has long been recognized in philosophical and moral traditions East and West (e.g. the Chinese concept of *ren*). The concept of personhood is central to discussions of human subjectivity, intersubjectivity (include relations with some animals), sociality and spirituality. Persons are real entities that are recognized in international law, human rights, the health sciences, and so on. But what does 'person' mean in these different contexts? This key concept has not been given the rigorous, consistent, theoretical clarification it requires. What is a person? Contemporary analytic approaches to personhood tend to be naturalistic (e.g. "animalism"), objectivist, reductionist, functionalist, eliminationist (as in eliminative materialism). Postmodern, trans-humanist and post-humanist approaches are also quite unsatisfactory and some are deeply worrying from an ethical standpoint. Some analytic metaphysics rely on mereological accounts or criteria of spatio-temporal continuity, or continuity of consciousness, and so on. Not one of these accounts seems to get to the heart of the complex, historically embedded way persons live, act, and die. The boundaries of personhood are also contested and disputes arise about who counts as persons. An acceptable theoretical account must lay down the essential interconnections between the key component concepts of personhood, namely, embodiment, consciousness (including affectivity, emotional engagement), selfhood and self-consciousness (which may come in degrees), rationality and agency, intersubjectivity and sociality. In this regard, I believe a phenomenological account can provide a unified theoretical framework for talking about persons as embodied *intentional meaning-makers* cooperating and interacting with each other to constitute a shared, meaningful world (Lynne Rudder Baker's account comes closest to a phenomenological account although she has limitations due to her naturalistic starting point). A rich, holistic and layered concept of personhood (which acknowledges the unique integrity as well as the temporally lived-through and experienced *historicity* of persons, embedded in a context with a meaningful sense of past and future) presents a radical challenge to the more compartmentalized, modular approaches to consciousness and cognition that are regularly encountered in contemporary philosophy of mind and in the cognitive sciences and neurosciences (Moran 2014b).

Finally, I think Husserl and Heidegger, especially, correctly diagnosed the modern age as an age of scientific technicity. The question of the meaning of this technological mode of living is profoundly relevant and even urgent for human existence in an age of environmental degradation. Phenomenology has made a significant contribution to emphasizing the "worldhood of the world" and thereby offers the possibility of underpinning environmental concerns with a proper account of human existence in the *Lebenswelt*.

15
Tetsuya Sakakibara

Professor of Philosophy

Graduate School of Humanities and Sociology, University of Tokyo (Japan)

---

1. Why were you initially drawn to phenomenology?

First of all, I would like to explain how I was initially drawn to *philosophy*. When I was a high school student preparing for an entrance exam at the university – around 1976 and 1977 –, the influence of the 1968-69 student movements was still noticeable here and there in Japan. It was not difficult to find people in high schools and universities who believed in Marxism and the possibility or even necessity of radical reform of our society. I was still at an impressionable age, and to say that I was not influenced by those people and ideas at all would certainly be not true at all. I still remember that I read some works by Marx and Engels in Japanese translations.

After entering university, however, I came to think that, in order to make an issue out of the society, it would rather be necessary to look at my own feet as well as closely into myself. Just around that time, I began to read Descartes' *Discours de la méthod*, *Meditationes de prima philosophia*, and Kant's *Kritik der reinen Vernunft*. These works showed me that only looking into oneself could lead to a sufficient understanding of the world. I thus decided to learn *philosophy* thoroughly.

In the second half of my undergraduate period, I read Kant's *Kritik der reinen Vernunft* more intensively. It seemed to me, however, that Kant certainly shows the apriori structure of the subject, which recognizes the world, but that he does not explain clearly how this structure is recognized. That is, Kant lacks reflection upon how the reflection upon the subjectivity is carried out. Just around the time I noticed that, I encountered Husserl's *Ideen I*. Husserl not only reflects upon and describes the noetic-noematic structure of the pure consciousness or transcendental subjectivity in which the world becomes constituted and appears with meaning, but also tries to reflect upon and describe this reflection itself. I, thus, wrote a graduation thesis on "The concepts of lived experience and reflection in Husserl's phenomenology" (in Japanese, unpublished, 1983), and decided to study *phenomenology* further in graduate school.

2. What are your main contributions to the field of phenomenology?

I have been engaged in research mainly on the problems of reflection and method in Husserl's phenomenology, and published a book on *The Genesis of Husserl's Phenomenology: An Investigation into the Establishment and Development of Its Method* [*Husserl Genshogaku no Seisei: Houhou no Seiritsu to Tenkai*] (University of Tokyo Press, Tokyo, 2009, in Japanese). This book represents the culmination of more than twenty-five years research about Husserl. Through intensive reading of Husserl's published as well as unpublished texts from his early stages toward the very end of his life, I clarified how the methods of phenomenological reduction and essential intuition, which should be required if a phenomenological reflection upon the consciousness or subjectivity is to be carried out, are established and developed in Husserl's phenomenology. Generally, phenomenology is well known for the motto "Zu den Sachen selbst!" which Heidegger discusses in *Sein und Zeit* (§ 7). My research elucidates, however, that the methods of phenomenology leading "zu den Sachen selbst" were rather gradually formed and developed "von den Sachen selbst her," that is, by being motivated by the matters themselves step by step.

This book has been written in Japanese, but several topics, which were discussed in it, are also argued in a number of my German and English articles. I will introduce one of them in detail.

The article I will present here, is "Das Problem des Ich und der Ursprung der genetischen Phänomenologie bei Husserl" published in *Husserl Studies*, Vol. 14, No. 1, 1997, pp. 21-39. By studying the original manuscripts of *Ideen II* in the Husserl Archives in Leuven and Cologne, I have been able to clarify in this article that Husserl, who had first acknowledged the possibility of phenomenological description of the pure Ego in his pencil-manuscripts of *Ideen I* (September and October 1912) and tried the description in his original pencil-manuscripts of *Ideen II* (October to December 1912) by following the method formulated in *Ideen I*, already faced a new matter, which crosses the range of this method, that is, the matter of the pure Ego which is, as identical subject, a temporal entity [*zeitlich Seiendes*] and lasts through its separate *cogitationes*. I argued that the description of this matter is nothing other than a slight, yet crucial, step to the genetic phenomenology in Husserl.

As it is well known, *Ideen II* comprises originally the texts, which Edith Stein and then Ludwig Landgrebe edited substantially on the base of Husserl's original manuscripts while Husserl was still alive, but after his death, they were first published as the fourth volume of *Husserliana* in 1952. After that publication, hardly anyone took notice of those original manuscripts of *Ideen II*. My article showed, however, the significance of these original manuscripts in order to elucidate the process of development of Husserl's thoughts up to the *genetic phenomenology*. It came to my knowledge that this caused a new edition of the original manuscripts of *Ideen II* and *Ideen III* in the Husserliana series, which is currently under progress in the Husserl Archives in Cologne. I think this is one of my main research contributions to the field of Husserl's phenomenology.

My article on "Struktur und Genesis der Fremderfahrung bei Edmund Husserl" (*Husserl Studies*, Vol. 24, No. 1, 2008, pp. 1-14), which interprets the complicated texts of Husserl's *Fünfte Cartesianische Meditation* by comparing the descriptions of static phenomenology with those of genetic phenomenology, and the article on "Reflection upon the Living Present and the Primal Consciousness in Husserl's Phenomenology" (in: Dieter Lohmar and Ichiro Yamaguchi (eds.), *On Time – New Contributions to the Husserlian Phenomenology of Time*, Phaenomenologica 197, Springer, Dordrecht / Heidelberg / London / New York, 2010, pp. 251-271), which elucidates a relationship between time, reflection, and the Ego in the so-called C-Manuscripts, can also be named as my more substantial research contributions to the field of phenomenology.

I would like to add that an English translation of the book mentioned above is now in progress and expected to be published in the near future.

3. What is the proper role of phenomenology in relation to other disciplines?

I think the answer will depend on what the term "other disciplines" could be taken to be. Here, I will try to answer this question from a perspective of my recent research interests.

Actually, by now I have been interested in *phenomenological research of nursing care* and engaged in a foundation and development of the *phenomenology of caring* for more than fifteen years. The result of my research includes "Phenomenological Research of Nursing and Its Method" (in: *Schutzian Research*, Vol. 4, 2012, pp. 133-150) and „Die Intentionalität der Pflegehandlung" (in: *Phänomenologische Forschungen, Jahrgang 2013, Soziale Erfahrung*, Felix Meiner Verlag, 2013, S. 249-265). I think that some proper features of phenomenology in relation to other disciplines will be clarified in the process of comparing the phenomenological method with other scientific methods in the research field of nursing care.

I will give an example and explain this point. Yumi Nishimura's work on *The Telling Body – A Phenomenology of Nursing Care* [*Katarikakeru Shintai – Kango Care no Genshogaku*] (Yumiru Shuppan, Tokyo, 2001, in Japanese) is an excellent piece of phenomenological research of nursing care, especially for patients in a "persistent vegetative state," which is defined in medical diagnosis as the state in which, although the patients open their eyes as if they had clear consciousness, their mental activities, such as the ability to respond to external stimuli or to recognize people or objects, cannot be confirmed, and they cannot communicate with the external world. Nishimura takes a keen interest in "a relationship and communication between a vegetative state patient and a primary nurse which cannot be grasped explicitly" and yet "exists," and tries to elucidate this matter. The relationship between the patient and the nurse cannot be observed from the outside by a natural-scientific method of clinical physiology. On the other side, the relationship cannot be grasped by the so-called "grounded theory approach" either. This method, as the most famous (and perhaps most used) qualitative research method, will analyze and validate a social human relationship by coding and categorizing the data collected through observations and descriptions and also by constant comparison in this process. But Nishimura points out that the grounded theory can *only* conceptualize *the conscious dimension perceived or realized by observation or description* and cannot reach the person's way of being that is not able to be grasped explicitly. Nishimura's matter is precisely a bodily, preconscious experience lived by the primary nurse, i.e., an experience of which the nurse cannot be explicitly conscious and yet, which has a meaning for the nurse. Thus, led by that matter itself, Nishimura comes to refer to Merleau-Ponty's phenomenology of the lived body, especially to his concept of "intercorporeity [*intercorporéité*]." According to Merleau-Ponty, in the bodily prelinguistic and preconscious stratum where mind and body are not yet separate, our bodies are communicating with each other by the "motor intentionality [*intentionnalité motrice*]" functioning in a reversible way. Based on this idea of our bodies' way of being proposed by Merleau-Ponty, Nishimura clarifies a primary nurse's meaningful experiences of/with her vegetative state patients, such as "twining of lines of sight" or "remaining a feeling of the patient's hand" in a compelling way.

Now, at least in the research field of nursing care, a proper feature of phenomenology in relation to other disciplines can be characterized in the following way: Differently from the natural-scientific method with observation and measurement from the outside, the phenomenological method investigates human meaningful experiences, which cannot be observed from the outside. But the proper feature of phenomenology, which is different from other qualitative research methods thematizing also human experiences is, that phenomenology elucidates the structure and genesis of these meaningful experiences from the fundamental structure of a human being, i.e., the intentionality of consciousness or lived body, or the care [*Sorge*] of Dasein, which cannot be disclosed by natural sciences but only by philosophy.

4. What have been the most significant advances in phenomenology?

If the proper role of phenomenology in relation to other disciplines can be characterized as mentioned above, then one of the most significant advances in phenomenology could be the fact that phenomenology has not only clarified the static intentional structure of meaningful experiences, but also come to elucidate their temporal genesis, in a word, *a development of the static phenomenology into the genetic phenomenology*. In my opinion, the late Husserl thematizes two kinds of "genesis": the one is the genesis in the *temporalized* [*gezeitigt*] level of temporality, as argued in his manuscript on "The Origin of Geometry"; the other and deeper one is the genesis as the *temporalizing* [*Zeitigen*] in every living present, which is disclosed in the so-called C-manuscripts. In my book stated above, I call the latter a "living genesis" and elucidate its dynamic "temporalizing-temporalized [*zeitigend-gezeitigt*]" structure. It seems to me that the very concept of this living genesis has been inherited by Merleau-Ponty. He characterizes phenomenology as the "will to grasp the sense of the world or of the history in its nascent state [*volonté de saisir le sens du monde ou de l'histoire à l'état naissant*]" (*Phénoménologie de la perception*, 1945, p. xvi). That way, phenomenology has been developed into the genetic phenomenology, which can elucidate the "genesis" of meaningful experiences in two different levels. I think this is, at least, one of the most significant advances in phenomenology.

5. What are the most important open problems in phenomenology and what are the prospects for progress?

Phenomenology has originated and developed as a philosophy, which clarifies the structure and genesis of meaningful phenomena or experiences by inquiring back to the performance of subjectivity that functions, so to speak, on this side of the phenomena, such as the intentionality of consciousness (Husserl), the care of Dasein (Heidegger), or the intentionality of the lived body (Merleau-Ponty). As the phenomenological investigation into the structure and genesis developed further, however, it has gradually become clear that, what constitutes the meaningful phenomena lies not only on this side but also beyond the phenomena (on the side of the world, as it were), and this is the case not only for Husserl but also Heidegger and Merleau-Ponty. An "unconscious" structure of the world, so to speak, which can never be disclosed by inquiring back onto this side of the phenomena – how can phenomenology elucidate such matters, which are lurking on or beyond the borders [*Grenzen*] of phenomenology? This could be one of the most important open problems in phenomenology.

For a future development of phenomenology, it is essential, in my view, to set up a new phenomenological description and analysis from concrete matters themselves – without applying the knowledge of the traditional phenomenology – and to clarify the method of this description and analysis. I will explain this point based on the phenomenology of caring which I am now engaged in.

Nursing care practice is really diverse and includes various interesting and rich contents and moments, which cannot be sufficiently elucidated by only applying the traditional phenomenology. For instance, nurses care for the patients and their families by forming a team and taking information and understandings from their colleagues, and by using various medical equipments in the situation changing minute by minute. Such practice of the nurses includes not just a few moments, which cannot be sufficiently explained with the concepts of "concern [*Besorgen*]" and "solicitude [*Fürsorge*]", which Heidegger determines in *Sein und Zeit*. Another example is the case that an expert nurse noticed the fact that the nurse-call did not ring although it should have and rushed to the patient. This case indicates that the intention of consciousness can direct itself to the absence of the data of sensation, which, to the best of my knowledge, Husserl never pointed out. Furthermore, Japanese nurses often use a pair of verbs, "*mukiau*" and "*yorisou*," in order to express their goal of nursing care. "*Mukiau*" means "face each other," therefore a relationship between I and Thou, but there is hardly an adequate English translation for "*yorisou*". Possible translations could be "stay close and go together," "be with someone's heart," or "accompany," but they are not sufficient yet. I feel that the nursing care practice of "*yorisou*" includes some elements, which Western philosophy has never investigated in its history.

The phenomenology of caring is not a mere application of the traditional phenomenology to the research of nursing care, but rather an attempt of revision and renewal of the traditional phenomenology itself *on the basis of and in terms of the matters themselves* in the field of nursing care. I hope that the future development of the phenomenology of caring will lead to a further development of phenomenology itself.

16
Anthony J. Steinbock

Professor of Philosophy, Director of the Phenomenology Research Center

Southern Illinois University Carbondale (U.S.A.)

---

1. Why were you initially drawn to phenomenology?

In terms of my philosophical background, I came to philosophy from two directions, namely, from academic and aesthetic inspirations. On the one hand, I was pointed in this direction through my studies and interests in both theology and geology. Looking back, but without knowing it at the time, this dual interest was probably an attempt to get "spirit" and "earth" or "body" together. Phenomenology is certainly a reflective approach to experience that traditionally attempts to overcome a dualistic kind of thinking.

On the other hand, I was led to philosophy, and to phenomenological philosophy in particular, through my training as a dancer, first in the classical Western tradition, and then in the more experimental vein of Nikolais Dance Theatre. More specifically, it was during training sessions with Nikolais and experiments concerning the constitution of space and time through movement that I simultaneously encountered similar ideas in Edmund Husserl, Max Scheler, Martin Heidegger, and especially, Maurice Merleau-Ponty. The latter took place when I was enrolled in a required introductory philosophy course with Professor Art Luther—someone who has remained a lifetime friend. For me, the meeting point of dance and philosophy was the reflective attentiveness to the spontaneous emergence of sense and meaning, and our participation in and responsibility for that dynamic process. Although I saw this taking place in dance and in literature, I found this expressed in very incisive and exciting ways in a phenomenological style of thinking.

2. What are your main contributions to the field of phenomenology?

Generally speaking, my main contributions in phenomenology concern the problem of evidence. Implicit in a phenomenological style of philosophy is the insight not only that "something" is given, and that this something has peculiar structures, or that there is "evidence," but also that there are many kinds of givenness and evidence, depending upon how we "accept" these matters and how they give themselves. In principle, this phenomenological openness to the things themselves requires an openness on our part to all matters, no matter how they give themselves, even if those matters and those ways of givenness seem to go against our usual patterns of thought and convictions.

The latter insight tended to be more implicit in Husserl, and carried out more descriptively than reflectively in his work. It is a more explicit and systematic point in Max Scheler, and it is taken up in various ways in subsequent figures like Adolf Reinach, Martin Heidegger, Emmanuel Levinas, Jean-Luc Marion, and Michel Henry. The difficulty is that only one kind of givenness has been privileged in phenomenology, and in philosophical thinking more generally. This kind of givenness I have called "presentation." My main contributions are related to exploring a broader realm of givenness, and to calling attention to, describing, and elaborating upon distinctive spheres of evidence.

Initially, I approached this broader sphere of evidence through Husserl with the formulation of a generative phenomenology and the different kinds of phenomena that a generative phenomenology could handle. "Generative phenomenology" was not explicitly formulated as such by Husserl in his published or unpublished work. When I undertook my studies of Husserl, I found that he had begun describing phenomena that went beyond genetic phenomena and what a genetic phenomenology could encompass. These phenomena included "homeworld," "alienworld," birth and death as constitutive features, historicity, narrative constitution, ritual, the role of animals as "co-companions," etc. In fact, he alluded to some of these features as "generative phenomena." Thus, I began detecting a movement here similar to what I found happening implicitly in the formulation of a static and genetic method as evidenced, e.g., in his lectures on transcendental logic in relation to his transcendental aesthetic.[1] In these later writings, he was beginning to describe phenomena that surpassed the limits of the genetic method, although he had not developed explicitly a new methodology that permitted such a description.

My task, in part, was to formulate a "generative phenomenology." Even though Husserl never used this expression, everything in Husserl suggested the formulation of a generative phenomenology. In some sense generative phenomenology had to have been implicitly present in Husserl from the very beginning—it had to be in order to describe what

---

[1] Edmund Husserl: *Analyses Concerning Passive and Active Synthesis: Lectures on Transcendental Logic*, trans., Anthony J. Steinbock (Dordrecht: Kluwer Academic Publishers, 2001).

he was describing; in another sense, generative phenomenology "only" emerged as such with *Home and Beyond*: hence the subtitle in *Home and Beyond*, namely, "Generative Phenomenology *after* Husserl."[2] It is after Husserl in the sense of "according to" Husserl, and it is after Husserl in the sense that it is formulated—and in some sense can only be formulated—temporally or historically after Husserl. But I want to be careful here and suggest that Husserl was already far ahead of himself. Working "after" Husserl in this way, also makes us generative phenomenologists, because we also generate the meaning of phenomenology and the meaning of generativity.

Furthermore, I understood generative phenomenology in two senses. First, by following out the internal movement of method in Husserl's thought, I traced three dimensions of method that corresponded to three dimensions of experience: static, genetic, and generative. In this respect, generativity and generative phenomenology were portrayed as one ever-deepening dimension among others (namely, among static matters and method, and genetic matters and method). Accordingly, generative method covers various trans-generational "generative" phenomena that are geo-historical, social, and normatively significant.

But generativity and generative phenomenology also had a more fundamental sense. In this case, I understood Generativity as the very movement itself from which emerges the relation: home/alien. Generativity is realized, as it were, only in and through this relation; "it" is the dynamic tension; "it" is the "new" absolute in Husserl. Properly speaking, then, generative phenomenology moves within the generative movement as it attempts to grasp the generative movement/Generativity. In this way, generative phenomenology describes Generativity from within Generativity, that is, within the generative movement itself.

In subsequent works, I have been elaborating upon "Generativity" and different kinds of givenness in what I have termed, "vertical" givenness. Modes of vertical givenness designate kinds of givenness that have their own styles of evidence, modalizations, verifications, etc., which are distinctive from the kind of givenness with which we tend to be most familiar, namely, "presentation"; they refer to cognitive dimensions that are irreducible to the ways in which sense and meaning are given in perception and judicative acts. These modes of vertical givenness bear on a variety of dimensions of human experience: a religious dimension of experience (the experience of holiness, for example, namely, "epiphany"); a moral dimension of experience (the experience of other persons, and oneself as person, that is, "revelation"); the expe-

---

[2] Anthony J. Steinbock, *Home and Beyond: Generative Phenomenology after Husserl*, (Evanston, Il: Northwestern University Press, 1995).

rience of objects as icons (manifestation), an aesthetic dimension of experience (distinct from embodiment, which I call provisionally at least, "exposure"), a dimension of experience where the Earth as ground is concerned ("disclosure"), and the experience of elemental beings as of the "earth" (namely, "display"). They all have their distinctive manners of givenness, and de-limit (that is, give, point to, and open up to other modes of givenness—the ecological to the holy to the moral, etc.) in their own ways—in ways that are distinctive from the givenness of objects in perception or reason, broadly construed.

Such different modes of vertical givenness have become a more prominent concern beginning with *Phenomenology and Mysticism: The Verticality of Religious Experience* (2007/2009)[3] and extended in *Moral Emotions: Reclaiming the Evidence of the Heart* (2014).[4] It is also one of the guiding concerns in my current works, *Beloved, Loving, and Hating*, and *Vocations and Exemplars: The Verticality of Moral Experience*.

For the most part, however, these other dimensions of experience tended to go unnoticed or denied, and granted little or no philosophical import. In *Phenomenology and Mysticism*, I described how the verification of religious experience is internal to its own kind of experiencing and occurs on this level of experiencing. Since the peculiar style of "cognition" and givenness concerning the sphere of the Holy, for example, does not conform to a rational style of evidence, its unique way of givenness, as well as its difficulties, its own kinds of deceptions, illusions, confirmations, etc., managed to be excluded in advance from philosophical consideration. However, perceptual evidence cannot authenticate spiritual experiencing; the experience of loving another or being loved by another can only be "confirmed," as it were, *within* that same kind of emotional experiencing, and not for example by rational reflection on the loving or any experiencing that is different *in kind*. Rather, it must be internal to or consistent with its own domain of experiencing.

I described this mode of vertical evidence ("epiphany") by exploring the first person narratives of three figures from the Christian, Jewish, and Islamic mystical traditions—St. Teresa of Avila, Rabbi Dov Baer, and Rūzbihān Baqlī, and by relating a broad range of religious experiences to philosophical problems of evidence, selfhood, and otherness. From this philosophical description of vertical experience, I developed

---

[3] Anthony J. Steinbock, *Phenomenology and Mysticism: The Verticality of Religious Experience* (Bloomington, IN: Indiana University Press, 2007/2009).

[4] Anthony J. Steinbock, *Moral Emotions: Reclaiming the Evidence of the Heart* (Evanston, IL: Northwestern University Press, 2014).

a social and cultural critique in terms of idolatry—as pride, secularism, and fundamentalism—and suggested that contemporary understandings of human experience must come from a fuller, more open view of religious experience.

Moral Emotions is a continuation of this project by calling attention to the emotional sphere of human persons, specifically through interpersonal emotions or the sphere of "moral" emotions. Having been customarily dismissed as having no evidential import, and being ultimately devoid of any of their own intrinsic spiritual, personal, or philosophical significance, the emotions generally speaking became reduced to merely subjective matters, devoid of any objective or rational grounding; they were systematically deemed within modernity to have no legitimate bearing on the purpose or meaning of human existence. This is why the project of the *Moral Emotions* is an attempt to "reclaim" the evidence of the "heart"—reclaim because the evidence of the heart has been present in Modernity, but relegated either to sensibility or placed under the dominion of reason.

Moral Emotions sought to do two main things: First, it attempted to give a fuller and richer account of the human person than is customarily available in interpretations that restrict evidence in human experience to the perceptual and judicative spheres merely. I did this by describing certain key "moral" or essentially interpersonal emotions. To bring these moral emotions into consideration in this way, I described them in original phenomenological analyses, paying attention both to how they give themselves in experience, as well as to their structural characteristics and interrelations. Such a critical perspective required an analysis of the emotions' modes of givenness (in relation to others, their temporal meanings and orientations, their possibility structures, their valences, etc.) and it required an attentiveness to how they can yield a broader sphere of evidence where persons are concerned.

My second aim was to show how the moral emotions can play a distinctive role in addressing the problems associated with modernity and those encountered at the impasse of postmodernity. The description of the moral emotions, as emotions of self-givenness (pride, shame, guilt), emotions of possibility (repentance, hope, despair), and emotions of otherness (trust, loving, humility), enabled me to suggest the ways in which they reveal unique dimensions of freedom, how they can take a leading role in shaping civic life and relations of power, and why the moral emotions should not be sidelined in such discussions. Since they can tell us about who we are as persons in concrete experiences, they can reveal novel aspects of freedom, normativity, power, and critique.

In this way, the moral emotions point to the possibility of contributing to the social imaginary of the modern and its postmodern variants, in a field where such interventions have been predominately guided by communicative ethics, rational theories of justice, the discourse of psychoanalysis and insights of bio-politics. In addition to pointing to different conceptions, for example, of freedom, normativity, and critique from the perspective of the moral emotions, one of my other conclusions in this regard concerned the way in which we understand the role of the emotions in the crisis of reason, modernity, and postmodernity, secularism and so-called "post-secularism." That is, if the moral emotions give us new insights into our social imaginaries, it is not because they constitute a new beginning (in relation to the old beginning of wonder, theory, or reason). Rather, it is because the emotions have been there all along, yet as subordinated in terms of what they are able to contribute; and it becomes a matter of recovering their distinctive contributions to who we are as persons, interpersonally. If there is a crisis, it is not in reason; nor is it a matter of coming back to the true sense of reason; rather, it concerns the way in which the emotions had lost—but should regain—their distinctive evidential footing.

3. What is the proper role of phenomenology in relation to other disciplines?

There is a prevalent ambiguity today when scholars and students speak of "phenomenology". It is often used as a synonym merely for "description". Sometimes it is implied as a first-person, introspective description, sometimes as a third-person quasi-objective description. Thus, we might hear today of a phenomenology of film, a phenomenology of tasting, a phenomenology of swimming, or a phenomenology of plant-life. With certain necessary qualifications, it is not that one cannot in principle embark on such enterprises phenomenologically. But phenomenology as I understand it has two main components: (1) it entails a description of *what* something is (as it is assumed to be), i.e., (a) a description of what something is as a "fact" or "in fact," and (b) a process of *ascertaining* structures that are more or less material, more or less formal, that is, essential structures of experience. (2) And it entails *how* this "what" is given; accordingly, it is a critical attentiveness to modes of givenness.

Given this initial clarification, it is possible to go further in explicating the relation between other disciplines that describe what something is and phenomenology's distinctive position. Evaluating the relation between phenomenology and other disciplines depends in part on the fields of study; moreover, the relation should be examined not only from the perspective of phenomenology's relation to other disciplines, but from other disciplines' relation to phenomenology. This relation is not a static one, but changes depending upon the matters under consideration. An interesting example can be found in the relation between ordinary language philosophy and phenomenology.

1. If we are examining something like tables and chairs, there might be a very limited rapport between something like ordinary language analysis and phenomenology. The former might give us no more than what we could describe with certain conceptual presuppositions bearing on perception, pragmatism, or Gestalt psychology. But if the problem field is more elusive, say, when considering the emotions, there can be a very fruitful relation between the two. In particular, ordinary language philosophy can circumscribe a meaning or meanings as starting points for further investigation, and it can do so via many cultures and languages.[5] In fact, one of the virtues of ordinary language philosophy is that it maintains its contact with everyday experience. The advantage of this approach is that it directly expresses everyday consciousness from the perspective of the lifeworld; it wants to reach understanding by examining the term in the conceptual contexts of its actual use. To the extent that it is descriptive, it returns to a living, engaged standpoint. As I mentioned, this is vital when examining something that can be as elusive as the emotions.

As I suggested in *Moral Emotions*, ordinary language philosophy can function as a "leading clue" to the critical elucidation of the phenomena (e.g., their temporal modes of givenness, their givenness of self, of other, etc.). It belongs as much to what we call a lifeworld ontology, as do psychology and anthropology. But it has a special resonance here because of its access to emotional experiences, an access that does not presuppose more complex theories and their substructions; it therefore can serve as a possible way into a more critical investigation. And phenomenology, especially generative phenomenology, does not ignore historical or linguistic presuppositions, but creatively works from them in an effort to elucidate those very experiences. In this way, phenomenology can work fruitfully with ordinary language philosophy. (I suspect that since Austin himself saw ordinary language philosophy as the first word, not the final word, and he himself was leaning toward calling what he did a kind of phenomenology, ordinary language philosophy might be able to accommodate phenomenology). This does not mean that ordinary language, like lifeworld ontologies, can substitute for a critical investigation, since phenomenology in its attentiveness to modes of givenness and structures of experience wants to clarify the very thing of which it takes advantage, namely, the pre-constituted familiar meanings and assertions about being. Rather, phenomenology brings the ordinary into view *as* ordinary which means that *as* ordinary,

---

[5] See *Moral Emotions*, "Introduction."

it is revealed as it fully is, which is to say, as anything but ordinary.

2. If hermeneutics is the discipline of interpretation within contexts, how does phenomenology pair with hermeneutics? Indeed, phenomenology, as generative phenomenology, should be especially attentive to the historical and interpersonal dimensions of meaning. Even when, for instance, we choose examples or exemplars as guides for our phenomenological constitutive and eidetic analyses, and as "authorities" or touchstones for these philosophical analyses, we encounter an unavoidable hermeneutical problematic in the sense of utilizing necessary presuppositions for a work that wants to mitigate assumptions and serve a critical philosophical analysis.

For me, it is not a question of the necessity of what we might generally call a hermeneutic enterprise, but rather of the place of that enterprise vis-à-vis phenomenology. There is an important distinction to be made between (1) a phenomenological hermeneutics, in which the main task is a hermeneutical one and whereby phenomenology serves to qualify it, and (2) a hermeneutical phenomenology in which hermeneutics serves the phenomenological enterprise concerning the clarification of sense and meaning constitution, and through this, the ascertaining of essential structures. My own approach regarding these two possibilities is the latter, namely, and a hermeneutical phenomenology, where the final court of appeal is the relation to experience, and thereby the clarification of its modes of givenness and structures.

3. Moreover, it is important to consider phenomenology in relation to first, second, and third-person accounts. Certainly, first-person descriptions have a privilege for phenomenology because of its distinctive access to experience. But second-person accounts can also be instructive in a phenomenological investigation. (I am not considering the possibility here of another person revealing me to myself through the emotional experience of loving, through which another may know me better than I know myself—thus gaining access to myself through a second-person perspective—but the possibility of first-person accounts that originate for me from another's narrations).

The fact that first-person accounts can stem for me from others and not from myself should not be taken as an impediment to description, but as an opportunity for another kind of access. This is an issue for the use of exemplars in phenomenology. It is not clear, in fact, that the description of our own first-person experiences demand any less critical examination than the description of the first-person description by others. Even my own descriptions of my first-person experiences are distanced reflections on my own experiences, and to this extent they may well coincide with other's reflections on my experiences. As I suggested in *Phenomenology and Mysticism*, while it is true that my descriptions of my bodily movements are distinct from others' descriptions of their bodily movements, phenomenology, as a cooperative effort, never excluded others' first-person accounts in an effort to clarify the phenomena. Phenomenology, instead, does not wish for third-person accounts of our lifeworld to wear the mask of truth, to parade as self-subsistent, neutrally objective, and thereby to dominate the field of lived-experiences. I do not have to have had the experience of a phantom limb, as we see described in Merleau-Ponty's *Phenomenology of Perception*, in order to give a phenomenological account of it as an ambivalent presence in the global kinesthesis of the lived-body and my being in the world.

This is not to say that third-person accounts cannot be useful or significant for or within a phenomenological undertaking. Contemporary research and collaborative efforts between phenomenology and cognitive science have shown this. In many ways, phenomenologists are doing today vis-à-vis the cognitive science what Merleau-Ponty was doing in his day with respect to experimental psychology. But here, what phenomenology brings to the table is precisely its conceptual apparatus developed now for over a century, distinctions concerning cognition, insights into lived-experience, the emplacement of the perceiver in the field of the perceived, as well as the overall critical and self-critical perspective in relation to the given. Phenomenology becomes the reflective posture that brings the world into its constitutive focus.

4. Let me return to the question of other disciplines that are "descriptive" and that in their own way "show". Insofar as other disciplines are descriptive of experience, they may have much in common with phenomenology. But insofar as phenomenology is not only a reflective posture, not only eidetic (or ontological) analysis, but also a critical one in the sense of giving an account of sense constitution and the genesis/generativity of sense and meaning, then phenomenology has a unique position among disciplines in terms of the description and evocation of sense and meaning.

How does phenomenology compare with the arts, or how do the arts compare with it—especially those forms of art that (also) do not want to take experience for granted? In the realm of film, for example, Ingmar Bergman, and others like him, explicitly understand that his endeavors – by working with detail, in images, with light, in time, the use of exemplars, etc. – are not produced as mere entertainment, but are undertaken to evoke the meaning of the human being at its most radical core. Like phenomenology, one could argue, the description of meaning is the revelation of meaning, and thus a creative enterprise.

In this case, we have at least two distinctive ways of disposing ourselves to the matters as they give themselves, and of creatively revealing that meaning as ushering it into existence. Here, the efforts of a film director and of a phenomenologist can cooperate or dovetail with each other, possibly without one ever knowing that the other is "cooperating" in this way. It is quite possible, then, that phenomenological philosophy does through Husserl, in the *realm of thought*, what film in the hands of Bergman does in the *realm of images and time*. But I want to be clear: film is not phenomenology, and phenomenology is not film. There is no point in reducing one to the other, to assert that there be a phenomenology "of" film or a phenomenology of the experience of film in order to give the latter validity. They can both be "revealing" disciplines that can work independently—in a superficial sense—and yet cooperatively without reducing phenomenology to film or film to phenomenology, despite their sometimes intriguing similarities.

4. What have been the most significant advances in phenomenology?

This is a difficult question for three reasons: first, because it raises the question concerning whether advances are at all possible in phenomenology; second, related to this, because it raises the question concerning different conceptions of phenomenology; third, and in a still related manner, because it is not possible to separate the question concerning the most significant advances *in* phenomenology from the question concerning the most significant advances *of* phenomenology. That is, given that we can speak of phenomenology as an established area of methodology and research, its subsequent "advances" "within" phenomenology also shape phenomenology *as* phenomenology and the advances "of" phenomenology.

In order to approach this issue, allow me to proffer in the form of a brief summary at least four points of significant contrast between phenomenology as a Hegelian "phenomenology of spirit," and a Husserlian "generative phenomenology."[6]

First, a Hegelian "phenomenology of spirit" only requires one phenomenologist in the sense of *any*-one indeterminate phenomenological philosopher. This is because the phenomenologist of spirit stands at the end of the emergence of all of the meaning-structures that have and could have appeared historically, and has described them exhaustively. In principle, only one (any-one) is required. But since the generative phenomenologist and phenomenology stand within a specific historicity or specific historicities (within the historical development of homeworlds to alienworlds), the singularity of the generative phenomenologist is essential: As the historicity of the situation changes, the

---

[6] See Anthony J. Steinbock, "Limit-Phenomena and Phenomenology" in Husserl (London: Rowman & Littlefield, 2017), ch. 4.

phenomenologist must critically describe and normatively participate in the generation of intersubjective and historical life. Moreover, the phenomenologist must continually account for the changes that she or he introduces into Generativity, and this in principle requires the generation of phenomenologists and generations of phenomenologists.

Second, the Hegelian phenomenologist at most can only describe new *factual and factical* events that express the *same meaning-structures* that have already been accomplished. Or put differently, any subsequent phenomenologist would only have the task of *repeating* or imitatively working through what the first phenomenologist already observed retrospectively. At most he or she would describe the repetition of meaning-shapes in new events. Moreover, if for Hegel all the meaning-structures had not been exhausted, it would still remain a question whether the phenomenologist would be involved in the generation of new meaning-structures, and whether there would be any occasion at all for the phenomenologist to appear on the scene. For Hegel places the phenomenologist at the historical, i.e., experiential completion of those shapes, and from the standpoint of non-experiential knowing, and in this sense (but only in this sense) at the "end of time." Accordingly, it is impossible for the Hegelian phenomenologist of spirit to experience crises and the possible transformation of meaning. There could be no advances in phenomenology, for example.

For the generative phenomenologist, however, the structure of generativity precludes such a closure, either conceived of as an overcoming of alienness, or as an exhaustion of meaning structures. The generative phenomenologist—or more accurately—generative phenomenologists in their specificity, experience crises according to future possibilities and are consequently involved in the critical project of generating (and not merely repeating) meaning-structures. At the very least, generative phenomenology opens itself to the possibility of the generation of new meaning structures, and in this respect, the phenomenologist(s) can never appear at the "end of time."

Third, and related to the former points, because the project of a generative phenomenology is situated within generativity, generative phenomenology cannot end with Husserl in the way a phenomenology of spirit ends (and "must" end) with Hegel. That is, phenomenology is itself generated "after" Husserl as handed down and appropriated over the generations, and it develops according to the historicity of the times and in terms of the facticity of the individual phenomenologists. This raises the question concerning the essential structures that are emergent.

Finally, while there is something clearly identifiable as Hegelian phenomenology, by the time one reaches a "generative phenomenology", the attribution of phenomenology only to Husserl becomes more ambiguous. Factually, generative phenomenology was never "contained" fully within Husserl's writings. But more importantly—essentially we might say—in order for generative phenomenology to be generative phenomenology, it must go beyond being "Husserlian" phenomenology. I do not mean this in the sense that "Husserlian" phenomenology is defective, like Schutz, Habermas, Adorno, or even Ricoeur might use the term. Rather, it belongs to the very structure of generative phenomenology that it goes beyond itself. Perhaps this sheds new light on the oft-cited phrase that the phenomenologist is a perpetual beginner and on the contention that phenomenology is an unending task.

Thus, to presuppose advances "in" phenomenology could suggest in some way that phenomenology is a set, static discipline, whose parameters have been predefined, and further that we are working to fill in the blank spaces. But if these "advances" are simultaneously developments *of* phenomenology, then the situation becomes more complex, and more interesting, because we are working from the perspective of a generative phenomenology as a phenomenology of Generativity, and further, we as phenomenologists, are as Husserl writes doing phenomenology as "standing within Generativity."

Having said this, and *if* we mark by phenomenology, "Husserlian" phenomenology, then perhaps the most significant advances have been those that open and continue to open the realm of what phenomenology can treat. That is, the advances pertain not to any this or that thing or area, but to broadening what is most peculiar to phenomenology itself, namely, the various spheres of evidence. And for these advancements, we could look to those whom Paul Ricoeur has called "Husserl heretics"—the long list of those whom Husserl may have rebuffed, but who in their own ways remained true to the spirit of Husserlian phenomenology.

5. What are the most important open problems in phenomenology and what are the prospects for progress?

From what has been said, I find that some of the most important and open problems in phenomenology still remain the problem of givenness, the exploration of these modes of givenness, the matters pertaining to them, and their intricate interrelations. More specifically, this requires a philosophical anthropology that is neither monistic nor dualistic, and one that entails a treatment of reason and sensibility, but offers a view of personal being that is not exhausted by reason and sensibility. That is, what is required is a philosophical anthropology that is rooted in detailed phenomenological investigations that are open to all dimensions of the human person. Such a philosophical anthropology needs to address the role of the emotions in all spheres of existence, and an exploration of loving as the core of what it means to be person in relation to all these spheres of existence and kinds of being. This is a generative matter, whose exploration is intrinsically inexhaustible. To be sure, the recognition of the distinctive dimensions of experience presupposes the attentiveness to a certain kind of human self-understanding, self-knowing, and self-recognition as inter-human and interspecies knowing; but these modes of knowing are rooted ultimately in genuine self-loving as inter-Personal and interpersonal. This is an experiential issue that concerns knowing and creatively realizing who we are and how we are related to one another as persons and with all beings. In short, it opens the profound question of vocations and their interrelation.

17
Bernhard Waldenfels

Ruhr-Universität Bochum (Germany)
Stonehill College, Easton, MA, USA
Text revised by Donald Goodwin

RESPONSIVE PHENOMENOLOGY

1. Phenomenology as a Philosophy of Radical Experience

In my view phenomenology means first of all a philosophy of radical experience which does not only reflect on experience, but rather, as Kant puts it in his *Prolegomena*, arises from the "fruitful *bathos*", that is, from the lowlands of experience. This presupposes a strong concept of experience as introduced to the 20th century by Edmund Husserl together with William James and Henri Bergson. I mean by this a sort of experience not restricted to supplying mere materials to function as a data basis, as in early Vienna positivism, or elements for constructing perception, memory or the body, as in present-day constructivism. A strong kind of experience, as can be found in Aristotle and again in Hegel, means that orders arise from experience itself and that we do not pass through these experiences without being changed ourselves. However, modernity includes the insight that every order can be other than it is, which does not, however, mean that it can be randomly different. Hence Merleau-Ponty defines philosophy as the search for sense *in statu nascendi*. But in pursuing an enhanced form of radicalized experience I do not only repeat the old wish to touch the *rizōmata pantōn*, the roots of everything, which persists in Marx as well as in Husserl. What I have in mind is a sort of experience in which something happens that cannot be anticipated by any planning and which cannot be recovered by any reflection. Such an experience does not only meet with the alien, rather it becomes alien to itself. This idea has lead me step by step to a special variation of responsive phenomenology.

The most important authors, authors who have never ceased to challenge me, are Plato (with Nietzsche in the background), Husserl,

Merleau-Ponty, later on Levinas, and with certain restrictions Foucault and Derrida. But I must say that the philosopher who gave me my first taste of phenomenology and literally seduced me to phenomenology was Merleau-Ponty, whose last lectures I attended in 1960–61 at the Collège de France and whose writings I later translated, edited and commented. Cézanne and Proust also belonged to this development. In my book *Phänomenologie in Frankreich* (1983, 2nd ed. 1998), I presented an extensive discussion of the interdisciplinary character of phenomenology in France, which has had considerable influence on the further development of phenomenology and even on the currents of French structuralism, and from which I have greatly benefited. This book is complemented by two collections of articles dedicated to the exchange between German and French thought: *Deutsch-Französische Gedankengänge* (1995) and *Idiome des Denkens. Deutsch-Französische Gedankengänge II* (2005). In addition to this, my *Philosophisches Tagebuch* (Munich: Fink 2008), edited by Regula Giuliani, contains notes from my "intellectual workshop" dating from 1980 to 2005; here the genesis of ideas makes its way amidst the events that occur around us and the ideas that occur to us.

2. Getting into Phenomenology

I studied philosophy in Bonn, Innsbruck, Munich and Paris, supplemented by the study of psychology, classical philology and history. To begin with, I acquired a thorough foundation in classical Greek philosophy in the courses of Helmut Kuhn and Kurt von Fritz, two émigrés who had returned to Germany. They also supervised my dissertation, *Das sokratische Fragen* (Meisenheim, 1961), dealing with the Platonic art of dialogue, with Socrates at the center and Kierkegaard in the background. The *Anschauungskraft*, the force of intuition, typical of ancient Greek thought, turned out to be a good preparation for phenomenological research. But the real path to contemporary phenomenology was opened to me during my stimulating research stay in Paris where I learned from Paul Ricœur and above all from Maurice Merleau-Ponty. In my habilitation thesis, *Das Zwischenreich des Dialogs. Sozialphilosophische Untersuchungen in Anschluß an Edmund Husserl* (The Hague: Nijhoff, 1971), I tried to transform Husserl's egological, transcendental approach into a dialogical phenomenology based on intercorporeity. This means that I and the Other, my own and the alien are coeval. The 'between' (*Zwischen*) takes on various forms of intertwining (of *Ineinander*, of *entrelac*) and appears with changing shades in Buber, Husserl, Heidegger and Merleau-Ponty, but also in sociologists such as Norbert Elias or in psychiatrists such as Kimura Bin. This motif turned out to be particularly fruitful. It is strictly opposed to all thought in dualistic oppositions and digital yes–no alternatives, and it awakens a sense for shades and fine distinctions.

3. Bodily Behavior

In the following years I tried to continue Merleau-Ponty's *phenomenology of bodily existence and coexistence*. To this end I engaged in a non-behavioristic theory of behavior (*Der Spielraum des Verhaltens*, 1980) and a non-fundamentalist and plural theory of the lifeworld (*In den Netzen der Lebenswelt*, 1985, 3rd ed. 2005). Through Merleau-Ponty's early work *La structure du comportement*, which I translated at that time, I became familiar with the wealth of material of German Gestalt psychology and medical anthropology. Most of the authors were Jewish, for example Goldstein, Gelb, Katz, Köhler, Koffka, Lewin and Straus; they were expelled from Germany and their research results only returned to their home country slowly and in fragments. One of the most important mediators was Aron Gurwitsch, a Jewish-Lithuanian author who emigrated from Frankfurt via Paris to the US. After his death I came in close contact with his widow; they had both found a new home in the milieu of emigrants and at the New School in New York. For me and my generation, phenomenology was largely a philosophy returning from exile.

Important for me were the debates with Jürgen Habermas and the contact with the sociological writings of Alfred Schutz, George Herbert Mead, Erving Goffman and Harold Garfinkel, some of whom I met personally. At a series of sociological meetings organized by Thomas Luckmann and his assistants I became acquainted with current social research. Traces of these activities are to be found in the collection Übergänge which together with a sociologist, first Richard Grathoff, then Wolfgang Eßbach, I have edited for the Fink publishing house since 1983. Further, a series of debates with Marxism, stimulated by critical Marxists and dissidents from Eastern Europe, among them Mihály Vajda from the Lukács circle, Ilja Srubar from the Patočka circle and Polish disciples of Ingarden and Kolakowski, also merit mention. The debates took place in postgraduate courses organized at the Inter-University Centre of Dubrovnik over four years. These debates helped to release German phenomenology from its political abstinence and to conceive the life-world not only as a cradle of sense, but also as a place of social conflicts. The results were presented in four volumes entitled *Phänomenologie und Marxismus* (1977–79, partial Engl. transl. 1984) that I edited together with Jan M. Broekman from Belgium and Ante Pažanin from Yugoslavia. Even before the political turn in 1989 there were lively contacts with Eastern-European phenomenologists, frequently taking up older traditions. This set a good counterbalance to a unilateral Western orientation.

I became familiar with analytical philosophy in Munich through the Austrian philosopher Wolfgang Stegmüller; it helped me to sharpen the methodological instruments of phenomenology. However, the Anglo-Saxon linguistic turn was never really attractive for me after having studied Merleau-Ponty's phenomenology of language and the linguistics of Bühler, Saussure, Jakobson and Benveniste. Half of it could be taken for granted, namely the assumption that there are no pure intuitions, that everything we experience is shaped by sense structures and that we manifest our inner experience by verbal and bodily expressions. But the other half was always dubious in my view, namely the assumption that every phenomenon first has to pass through the filter of linguistic analysis and that sense of all kinds reaches us only packed in texts as if reading texts could replace looking at things. The psycholinguistics of Hans Hörmann, my colleague in Bochum, encouraged me. As to the theory of communication developed by the younger Frankfurt school, it seemed important to me to resist all attempts to degrade the pre-predicative and pre-normative structures of experience to mere pre-steps within a process of seeking consensus by arguments. My resistance to any sort of lingualism was supported by the dynamic structuralism of the Russian linguist Roman Jakobson. I became personally acquainted with him through Elmar Holenstein, his former assistant in Harvard, and I was highly impressed by his sensitive form of scholarship.

The initial step of my philosophical thought corresponds to a sort of *existential–structural phenomenology*, centered on a *plurality of reference and sense* and based on *corporeality*. In accordance with Husserl I take our body as a transfer point (*Umschlagstelle*) between the psychological and the physical, between sense and causality, but also between the own and the alien. Helmuth Plessner, who returned to Germany from Dutch exile, developed a theory of the body close to Merleau-Ponty's; being a body (*Leib-Sein*) and having a body (*Körper-Haben*) cross each other. The body as a place of self-reference, including references to the Other and a certain self-withdrawal, plays a crucial role in my phenomenology of otherness, which developed gradually. This process is documented by the volume *Das leibliche Selbst* (2000) which goes back to a series of lectures dealing with the bodily self.

4. Order in the Twilight

In the seventies I encountered the new vogue of French structuralism, which changed my philosophical orientation, but only to some extent. The problem of *order* became more and more important, especially in terms of limited and variable orders. In opposition to the comprehensive order of the cosmos and to the fundamental order of morals and law, limited orders are contingent through and through. There is order, *il y'a de l'ordre*, as Foucault puts it, but there is not one single order. In a similar way Merleau-Ponty had stated in his *Phenomenology of Perception* that *there is sense*, but not *sense as a whole*. Orders arise from a process of selection and exclusion, both occurring together. The incompossibility of heterogeneous formations generates forms of repugnance (*Widerstreit*) which cannot be settled by referring to sufficient reasons (*Ordnung im Zwielicht*, 1987, new edition Munich: Fink, 2013, Engl. *Order in the Twilight*, Ohio University Press, 1996). I was induced to choose this title by a theatre poster in Paris where the German title *Im Zwielicht* was rendered by *Entre chien et loup*. This reminds us of a dusky zone in which it is impossible to distinguish unequivocally between dog and wolf. In his book *La pensée sauvage*, dedicated to Merleau-Ponty, his former colleague at the Collège de France, Claude Lévi-Stauss takes the same course, referring to a threshold between culture and nature that we will never cross.

Assuming a sort of wild being and wild thought leads to a double problem. On the one hand we are confronted with the basic fact that experience only takes shape by *reducing a surplus of possibilities* or – to put in terms of system theory – by reducing complexity. There is always more that is possible than real. In his Vienna novel *Der Mann ohne Eigenschaften,* Robert Musil, who was also a reader of the early Husserl, advocates a sense of possibility transcending the sense of reality. But this only the one side. The mere pluralisation of possibilities and permanent code switching, propagated by what is called postmodernity, miss the fundamental fact that something has *to be seen* and *to be heard*, *to be said* and *to be done* which imposes itself upon us before we can make a choice. The grammatical form of the gerundive, which can be reduced neither to the indicative nor to the potentialis, indicates demands which, for lack of an encompassing order, appear as overdemands.

5. Response to the Other

Two central questions arise from this new problematic. On the one hand, we are confronted with the otherness or alienness (*Fremdheit*) of the Other, which functions like a sting. The Other's extra-ordinary demand (in German: *Anspruch*, which means both appeal and claim) goes beyond the limits of any personal and collective order (*Der Stachel des Fremden*, 1990, 3rd ed. 1998). On the other hand, there is the problem of how to deal with the Other's demand without silencing it by means of pre-given categories or norms. This problem seems to be solved by speaking *from the Other* before speaking *about the Other*. We fall into a kind of self-precedence, which makes us start from elsewhere. Starting from elsewhere, that is precisely what we do when we respond. In this context I use the term *responsivity* in the sense specified by the physician Kurt Goldstein. Apart from this Latin terminology we may speak of *Antwortlichkeit* in German, of *answerability* in English or of *otnetvost'* in Russian as Mikhail Bakhtin does in his studies on literature.

In my large-scale book *Antwortregister* (1994, Engl. *Responsive Register*, Northwestern, forthcoming) I continue my earlier dialogical investigations, but not without releasing them from the embrace of communicative reason. The one who demands and the other who responds are not in a symmetrical arrangement; there is no third party capable of bridging the gulf between demand and response. There is no dia-logue without interruption, as Maurice Blanchot clearly shows in his book *L'entretien infini*. The fundamental feature of responsivity as I propose it competes with the well-known phenomenological aspect of intentionality and the hermeneutic aspect of understanding; it does not all replace them, but it goes deeper.

What follows from this is a special logic of response. This logic has to do in the first place with the *singularity* of demands, which are beyond all limits. Take the patient's cry for help or the irruption of something new for which we have no words. Consider also the incomparability of the holocaust, which weighs so heavily on us Germans; this does not exclude singularity in the plural because there is no highest evil. The logic of response teaches us secondly that demands appear with a sort of *inevitability*; we *cannot not respond* just as, according to Paul Watzlawick, we *cannot not communicate*. Such a practical necessity evades the canonic disjunction of Is and Ought and the symmetrical distribution of rights and duties. As a third aspect, the *posteriority (Nachträglichkeit)* of responding has to be mentioned, due to the fact that the Other's demand arises from elsewhere and precedes our own initiative. In general, responding originates from a sort of *responsive difference*. That *to which* we respond exceeds *what* we answer. The event of responding and its content are separated from each other precisely as linguistics distinguishes between saying and what is said. What we respond is more or less up to us, but what is not up to us is that to which we have to respond.

Traditional differences such as transcendental/empirical, eidetic/factual, or ontological/ontic reach their limits. In elaborating this sort of responsive phenomenology, which irrevocably starts from the Other and from the Alien, my thought was close to Emmanuel Levinas in spite of some reserves. What comes out is not a separate form of ethics, but a kind of implicit ethics, bound up with the responsive character of experience.

6. Ruptures of Experience in Phenomenology, Psychoanalysis and Phenomenotechnique

The efforts to unfold a responsive sort of phenomenology continued in my next book, *Bruchlinien der Erfahrung. Phänomenologie, Psychoanalyse, Phänomenotechnik* (2002). The main rupture runs between *pathos* and *response*. Now the demand of the Other takes on more pathic and affective features. Our experience goes back to something by which we are touched *before* we respond.

Pathos and response are separated by a sort of *diastasis*, a peculiar sort of time-lag which temporalizes our experience in an unusual way. Experience that starts from something happening to us, from a sort of *Widerfahrnis*, precedes itself. The fragility of experience does not stop short of us ourselves. Our bodily self is a divided self; it appears in a double way, as a *patient* inasmuch as we are affected by something, and as a *respondent* inasmuch as we respond to that. To the extent that the self is permanently exposed to the Other's demand, gaze, gesture and desire, the Other appears as an original sort of *double*. As Merleau-Ponty and before him Valéry have shown, experience of oneself and experience of the Other are intertwined in a form of chiasma. We encounter in ourselves what is the Other's, and we encounter in the Other what is our own, but what is excluded is a complete coincidence.

While exploring the margins and abysses of our experience, phenomenology is challenged in a special way. Such challenges occupy the last two chapters of the *Bruchlinien*. On the one hand, phenomenology of consciousness and hermeneutics of existence are undermined by the subterranean work of *psychoanalysis*. Central issues such as the alienness of the unconscious, the unsettling effect of the uncanny, displacement and condensation in dream and neurosis, the bodily language of symptoms, traumatic after-effects, self-affection and Narcissism, family bonds or the transference within treatment require a phenomenological counter-reading to which authors such as Lacan, Laplanche, Pontalis, but also Binswanger and Maldiney have made significant contributions. The Sigmund-Freud-Stiftung in Frankfurt and a research circle moderated by Ilka Quindeau gave me the opportunity to discuss my own ideas with professional psychoanalysts.

On the other hand, the intervention of techniques is a substantial challenge to phenomenology. These techniques open new paths of *phenomeno-technique* and *somato-technique* which intervene in the process of sense-formation and self-formation. The operation of technique is not restricted to the use of secondary tools that help to realize pre-given and pre-posited aims. It is also not sufficient to invoke the power of technique with reference to Heidegger's *Ge-schick* and *Ge-stell*. Rather, we must try to locate technique, in its archaic and in its most modern forms, within our bodily experience. The starting point might be the question: How does our experience *function*. The 'how' of our experience can be reduced neither to objective structures and goals nor to subjective intentions and projects; it is precisely what Husserl and Heidegger thematize as signification or significance. However, there is not only a genuine "logos of the aesthetic world", as Husserl postulates, or a world of tools (*Zeug*), as Heidegger shows; there is a genuine techno-logos, displaying its effects in an intermediary world of tools, machines and apparatuses. New modes of biotechnology, amalgamating natural growth and artificial fabrication, approximate a borderline beyond which every therapeutic treatment of the Other is reduced to technological actions upon the Other. Models of *self*-organization and of *auto*-poiesis leave it open what such a 'self' means. The riddle of Descartes' *corpus meum* returns as a riddle of my brain. As Husserl postulates in his *Crisis*, phenomenologists should provide precise description so that we do not "take for true being what is actually a method"; otherwise significations would be reduced to mere "game meanings", and ultimately the brain would think for us as a neurological homunculus. One has to show how the brain co-operates with our bodily experience without replacing it. Neurophenomenology is not a solution, but a field of problems.

7. Dimensions of Alienness

The motive of otherness or alienness is divided into many facets. Otherness is not a special issue, but something like the salt pervading all our experience. This is the topic of the four-volume series *Studien des Fremden* (1997–99). The first volume, *Die Topographie des Fremden* (1997, 2nd ed. 1999), outlines the whole problem complex. It encompasses the paradox of ethnology as xenology, as a science of the alien, and also nationalistic and culturalistic, political and economic forms of appropriation. The second volume, *Grenzen der Normalisierung* (1998, augmented edition 2008), enters the areas of science, technique and politics. It moves between the normal, the anomalous and the pathological with reference to such authors as Schutz, Goldstein, Canguilhem and Foucault. The third volume, *Sinnesschwellen* (1999), considers the thresholds of our senses and especially the synesthetic and rhythmic interplay of our senses. Sensuous experience is both intensified and *verfremdet*, alienated, by the arts of pictures, of sounds and of architectonic space. Aisthesis and aesthetics are closely connected. The arts are places of practiced phenomenology. The fourth volume, *Vielstimmigkeit der Rede* (1999), shows, following Mikhail Bakhtin, how alienness pervades our own speech, turning every word into a "half-alien word". What we discover is not one great otherness, but a many-colored alienness.

The facets of alienness are related to contemporary debates by essays assembled under the title *Verfremdung der Moderne* (Göttingen: Wallstein, 2001). They are intended to give the "project of modernity" proclaimed by Jürgen Habermas a hypermodern spin. In the small book *Grundlinien einer Phänomenologie des Fremden* (2006, 4th ed. 2012, engl. *Phenomenology of the Alien*, Northwestern 2011) the key ideas are linked. In lectures delivered in Hong Kong and published there and in New York under the title *Question of the Other* (2007) the phenomenology of the alien takes on intercultural features.

8. Between Attention and Respect

Responsive phenomenology combines cognitive and practical aspects. The distance between the two is bridged by the phenomenon of attention which philosophers are inclined to treat peripherally, with the exception of Husserl, Bergson and James. In my book *Phänomenologie der Aufmerksamkeit* (2004) attention functions as a prime example of a pathic and responsive sort of phenomenology. Attention can be reduced neither to subjective acts nor to anonymous mechanisms, but rather oscillates between *Auffallen* and *Aufmerken*: something strikes me (*es fällt mir auf*) and I take notice (*ich merke auf*). Between the id (*Es*) and the ego (*Ich*) arises a field of gravitation that changes the "weight of things" (Nietzsche). We take part in what happens, but not as autonomous subjects. Something comes upon us and confronts us before we approach it. In psychoanalysis Freud recommends a "floating attention" (*gleichschwebende Aufmerksamkeit*) in order to outwit the resistance of the ego. The process of attention is further shaped by techniques, media and social practices that all together create an economy, a politics and a didactics of attention. Finally, attention touches upon the *respect* we render and owe to each other. In German there is a linguistic affinity between *Aufmerksamkeit* and *Achtung*, which means both attention and respect. Independently of such linguistic peculiarities, attention is marked by an ethical accent; it appears as the nucleus of an ethos of the senses.

In the next book, *Schattenrisse der Moral* (2006), I pursue this ethical line, looking for the shadows of moral. I confront Kant's law-like morals and Aristotle's ethics of virtue with a responsive ethics that transgresses the borders of aims and rules by responding to the Other's demand. This genealogy of morals, inspired by Nietzsche, revolves around a "blind spot of morals"; new light is shed on traditional issues such as freedom, right, power and violence. This opens a space for a specific time of ethos with the effect that there is something immemorial and unexpectable in all our recollections and expectations. We call ethical something that cannot remain indifferent even if we try to neutralize it.

The ethical difference, going beyond any eidetic or ontological difference, originates from a peculiar kind of "non-indifference", as Levinas puts it. This contests the nonchalance of somebody who declares, "it's all the same to me" (*mne wsjo rawno*), as does the ridiculous man in Dostoyevsky's story. This non-indifference can be understood as an ethical variant of *thaumazein;* it arises from the primary fact that there is somebody other.

9. Modalities and Paradoxes of Experience

Husserl already presents the experience of the alien pervading all our experience in a paradoxical way, speaking of the "accessibility of what is originally inaccessible" or of "accessibility in the mode of the incomprehensible". Paradoxes are inevitably produced by the fact that the beginning of our experience escapes us or by the fact that the limits of experience are inscribed into our experience like the horizons of experience that shift, but accompany us like our own shadow. The phenomenology of alienness opens immense fields of research. In the last years I have made several attempts to explore these fields. The result was four volumes: *Ortsverschiebungen, Zeitverschiebungen* (2009), *Sinne und Künste im Wechselspiel* (2010), *Hyperphänomene* (2012), *Sozialität und Alterität* (2015) in which various modes of experience were envisaged: modes of time–space experience, of aesthetic experience, of hyperbolic experience and of social experience.

My reflections on spatial and temporal displacements start from a paradoxical situation; we are at once *here and elsewhere, now and at other times*. The zero point of "here" and "now" is strictly speaking a non-place that can be located and dated only in an indirect way by using maps and calendars. This corresponds to the figure of Socrates characterized as the *atopos*, that is, the stranger who is never completely in place. Due to what is referred to as the return of space, geography has stepped out the shadow of historiography. The increasing tension between the local and the global calls for a bodily orientation which resists both extremes, the fixation on one's own "here" and the volatilization of the "here" leading to the "anywhere" of an endless globalization. Otherwise we are threatened by collective forms of claustrophobia and agoraphobia.

The senses and the arts are entangled with each other in various ways. The world of pictures, the world of sounds, the mobile art of dance, the scene of the theatre, the art of the kitchen and the table, and also the skill of pain treatment are *schools of senses* where we learn to see and to hear things we usually neglect. Camus' dictum *"rapprendere à voir* – to re-learn to see" is by no means obsolete. Bringing the arts closer to the pathos of the senses could preserve them from an aestheticist, an academic, a technical or a market-like artificiality.

Hyperphenomena are phenomena which are *more than they seem to be*. A corresponding form of hyperphenomenology emphasises the multiple surplus of experience. It comes close to the Platonic hyperbolics which in Book VI of the *Republic* passes "beyond being" (Levinas) and which is concealed by a Platonist doubling of the world.[1] Old motives such as infinity, impossibility, invisibility or the immemorial are rediscovered as means of incitement that prevent us from falling into the sleep of normality and from becoming what Nietzsche calls *Normalmenschen*, that is, humans who only function. Social phenomena such as the gift, trust or representation and even the excesses of violence appear in a new light when they are interpreted as social forms of self-transgression. Religious transcendence no longer conveys the impression of a mere *Hinterwelt* if the religious and the holy are understood as phenomena of alienness and otherness.

My recent reflections on social experience revolve around the Kantian paradox of an *unsocial sociality*. Alterity does not refer to the "totally Other". Rather, it refers to the incarnate Other who is involved in a net of roles, duties and rituals, but whose singularity is not absorbed in all that. The "with" of being with others, rediscovered but also foreshortened by Husserl and Heidegger, raises the question of a social bond which can be reduced neither to social contracts nor to mere conventions. The social comes forth in sensuous affects like anxiousness and shame, but also in social rituals accompanying birth, death and all threshold experiences. Even animals and things are more than mere things at our disposition; in spite of their particular alienness they are included in our corporeal being-with.

---

[1] As to this sort of reading Plato see my latest book: Platon. Zwischen Logos und Pathos (2017)

18

Dan Zahavi

Professor of Philosophy, Director of Center for Subjectivity Research,

Department of Media, Cognition, and Communication, University of Copenhagen (Denmark)

---

1. Why were you initially drawn to phenomenology?[1]

I met philosophy early. I read much as a child, and occasionally came across references to philosophy. I didn't understand what it meant, but I was curious, and when I was 12 years old, I asked my mother to buy me a copy of Will Durant's *The Story of Philosophy: the Lives and Opinions of the Greater Philosophers*. I can't claim to have understood much at that age, but Durant's account of Plato was still so inspiring that I there and then decided that I wanted to study philosophy. And that is a decision I have stuck to, and which I have never had cause to regret. It made me opt for modern languages in high school, since I wanted to learn German so that I could read Kant and study in Germany. Right after high school, I enrolled as a philosophy student at the University of Copenhagen. Already during the first year of study, I was briefly exposed to Husserl and Heidegger (reading excerpts from *Die Idee der Phänomenologie* and *Was ist Metaphysik?*). At that point, however, I was primarily interested in the history of philosophy and delved into Aristotle, Thomas Aquinas, Kant and Hegel. At some point, however, it started to dawn on me that Husserlian phenomenology in some way might be seen as a kind of synthesis between Aristotelianism and transcendental philosophy. So I decided to write my MA thesis on him, and at the same finally realize my old plans about studying abroad. I obtained a DAAD scholarship and went to Wuppertal in Germany to study with the renowned Husserl-scholar Klaus Held. Held had been the assistant of Landgrebe, who himself had been one of Husserl's assistants. In the spring of 1991, I handed in my MA thesis on Husserl's

---

[1] An earlier and rather different version of the present text originally appeared in Danish in F.K. Thomsen & J.v.H. Holtermann, eds. 2010. *Filosofi: 5 spørgsmål*. Automatic Press.

Logische Untersuchungen, which was entitled *Intentionalität und Konstitution*. It also became my first book (Zahavi 1992).

By then my path was pretty much set. I was able to obtain a PhD scholarship and went to the Husserl Archives at the *Katholieke Universiteit Leuven* in order to work with Rudolf Bernet as my doctoral supervisor. In 1994, I successfully defended my thesis *Husserl und die transzendentale Intersubjektivität*, which later was also published as a book (Zahavi 1996). After some years as post.doc and assistant professor (spent partially in Paris), and after having written and defended my habilitation *Self-awareness and alterity* (Zahavi 1999), I submitted an application to the *Danish National Research Foundation* together with two colleagues, Arne Grøn and Josef Parnas. The application was successful and in 2002 allowed me to establish the *Center for Subjectivity Research*, which I have directed since. In 2006, I obtained a permanent position as professor of philosophy at the University of Copenhagen. Whereas my own background is strictly in philosophy, and whereas I initially worked alone, and only with philosophy, after the establishment of the *Center for Subjectivity Research* I increasingly started to collaborate with other people, including empirical researchers such as the psychiatrist Josef Parnas, the clinical psychologist Louis Sass, the developmental psychologists Philippe Rochat and Vasudevi Reddy, and the neuroscientist Andreas Roepstorff. Philosophers I have collaborated with include Shaun Gallagher and Evan Thompson. Together with the latter two, for a number of years I have been involved in an attempt to build bridges between phenomenology, philosophy of mind, and cognitive science.

2. What are your main contributions to the field of phenomenology?

From the outset, I took it to be important to bring phenomenology into dialogue with other philosophical traditions. In my PhD, I drew on critical theory (Habermas), in my habilitation it was the Heidelberg school (Henrich and Frank) and analytic philosophy of language and philosophy of mind (in particular Rosenthal, Anscombe, Perry, Castañeda and Armstrong). After the *Center for Subjectivity Research* was established, my methodological and theoretical pluralism has only become ever more pronounced.

In my PhD, I presented a new interpretation of Husserl's theory of intersubjectivity. I argued that Husserl's main reason for dwelling so much on the topic of intersubjectivity was transcendentally motivated, and that his phenomenology would ultimately have to be appreciated as an intersubjective transformation of transcendental philosophy. In other words, rather than being interested in the basic building blocks of reality, Husserl was concerned with the transcendental philosophical question of what it means for something to be real, and how we can experience it as such. He defended the view that these questions could only be answered by considering the contribution of the intersubjective community. I also discussed Sartre's, Merleau-Ponty's and Heidegger's contribution to a phenomenological theory of intersubjectivity, and stressed the common features and virtues of such analyses when compared to the language-oriented approach to intersubjectivity found in Habermas and Apel. My PhD was published in the spring of 1996, a few months after Anthony Steinbock and Natalie Depraz had published their respective analyzes of Husserl's theory of intersubjectivity. The three books are all different, and deal with different aspects of Husserl's theory. But they are all characterized by drawing on a quite comprehensive amount of sources and by their rejection of the traditional reading of Husserl as a quasi-solipsist. Since then, all three of us have often been classified as representing a new generation of (revisionist) Husserl scholars. A more overarching presentation of my reinterpretation of Husserl – which responds to the widespread portray (caricature) of Husserl as a subjective idealist, intellectualist, immanentist etc. – can be found in the book *Husserl's Phenomenology* (Zahavi 2003a).

In my habilitation, I defended the concept of pre-reflective self-consciousness, i.e., the idea that our experiential life is characterized by a form of self-consciousness that is more primitive and more fundamental than the reflective form of self-consciousness that one, for instance, finds in various kinds of introspection. I presented a detailed reading of Husserl's analysis of self-consciousness and inner time-consciousness (which criticized Sokolowski's and Brough's internal object model), and demonstrated more generally, by also drawing on Merleau-Ponty, Sartre, Henry and Derrida, how central and fundamental a role the concept of self-consciousness plays in phenomenological philosophy. Phenomenology is not merely interested in the question of how consciousness is involved in the appearance of objects, but has precisely also inquired into the self-appearance of consciousness. The book is probably the most exhaustive discussion of phenomenological accounts of self-consciousness available, and was in 2000 awarded with the Edward Goodwin Ballard Prize in Phenomenology.

My research in the years that followed has continued to target the same basic issues. On the one hand, I have been preoccupied with the relationship between experience, self and self-consciousness. I have argued that all three concepts are interdependent and that a theory of consciousness that wishes to take the subjective dimension of our experiential life seriously needs to operate with a (minimal) concept of self. Opponents have included those who either deny the reality of the self or who claim that the self is a social construct whose formation requires language and concept use, normativity and narratives. As part of this work I have investigated the strengths and weaknesses of the narrative account of self, discussed and criticized various forms of self-skepticism, and examined some of the forms of self-disorders that we find in schizophrenia (cf. Zahavi 2003b, 2005, 2007a, Sass, Parnas, Zahavi 2011). During the last few years, this interest has also gone in a more intercultural direction. I have started to engage in discussion with experts in Buddhist philosophy from USA, UK and Australia, in order to explore the nature, structure and reality of self-awareness and selfhood (see Siderits, Thompson, Zahavi 2011).

On the other hand, I have continued to write on intersubjectivity, empathy and social cognition. I have defended a phenomenological account of empathy, argued in favor of the bodily and contextual character of interpersonal understanding and criticized dominant positions within the so-called 'theory of mind' debate, including simulations theory and theory-theory. As part of this work, I have also spent time discussing and criticizing some of the standard accounts of autism, including the claim that the reason why people with autism have difficulties understanding and interacting with others is due to deficiencies in their theoretical capacities (Zahavi 2001, 2008a, Zahavi & Parnas 2003).

In recent years, I have worked increasingly on social emotions (Zahavi 2010a). My interest has mainly been due to the fact that emotions like shame do not merely manifest a salient form of self-experience, but at the same time also involve relations to others. To that extent, they constitute important resources for a better understanding of the self-other relation. This work has gradually led me to the social ontology debate and to the question of how to understand shared emotions, we-experiences and collective identities. These are all topics that I will continue to work on in the coming years.

In parallel with my systematic work in these areas, I have continued my Husserl research, and, for instance, discussed the metaphysical implications of transcendental phenomenology: Can the phenomenological clarification of the lifeworld and of the structure of experience tell us something about the nature of reality itself (Zahavi 2008b)? At the same time, I have sought to establish and promote increasing cooperation between phenomenology, analytic philosophy of mind, and cognitive science (in particular development psychology and psychopathology). This latter effort was the main reason why I in 2006 was awarded the *Elite Research Prize* of the Danish Ministry of Science, Technology and Innovation. Three publications representative of this endeavor are the books *Subjectivity and Selfhood* from 2005, *The Phenomenological Mind* from 2008 (which is co-authored with Shaun Gallagher with whom I am also co-editing the journal *Phenomenology and the Cogni-*

tive Sciences), and *Self and Other: Exploring Subjectivity, Empathy and Shame* from 2014.

Although I initially largely identified myself as a Husserlian, I eventually found the disagreements that have marked the relations between the different traditions in phenomenology more and more counterproductive. It is not that it cannot be useful to focus on the difference between, for example, Husserl's, Heidegger's, Sartre's and Merleau-Ponty's understanding of phenomenology. But too much emphasis on the difference does not only run the risk of degenerating into a kind of trench war, which is anything but philosophical fruitful, it also weakens the effort to make phenomenology a powerful and systematically convincing voice in contemporary philosophy. For the same reason, in the last years I have been increasingly more eclectic in my use of the resources that can be found in phenomenology (cf. Zahavi 2003c, 2007b, 2008c). The same attitude has also characterized my work in the *Nordic Society for Phenomenology,* which I, together with Hans Ruin and Sara Heinämaa established in 2001, and which I was then president for during the following 6 years.

3. What is the proper role of phenomenology in relation to other disciplines?

This is a rather tricky question, and it is not possible to give a univocal answer. It not only depends on what disciplines we are talking about (e.g., other forms of philosophy or empirical science), but also on the kind of phenomenology in question. Let us recall the distinction between transcendental phenomenology, on the one hand, and Husserl's notion of phenomenological psychology or Schutz' notion of a phenomenology of the natural attitude, on the other. Briefly put, this is a distinction between a phenomenology with global aspirations, the aim of which is to address very fundamental philosophical questions (such as the nature and status of meaning, truth, and objectivity) and a phenomenology with a more local or circumscribed focus that describes and analyzes a variety of concrete phenomena, be it specific forms of intentionality or certain structures of the life-world. When it comes to the former kind of phenomenology, it should find its place among related and competing philosophical accounts. When it comes to the latter, I think phenomenology is in a position to offer important resources to a variety of empirical disciplines. When phenomenology investigates basic forms of social interaction, the role of embodiment in perception, the nature of self-consciousness, various social stratifications, etc., it is exploring topics that are also discussed in and investigated by a variety of non-philosophical disciplines including developmental psychology, cognitive psychology, anthropology, sociology, psychiatry and neuroscience. Importantly, this does not merely entail that phenomenology might contribute with its own careful descriptions of the explanandum. It can also have an impact by questioning and elucidating basic theoretical assumptions made by empirical science, just as it might aid in the development of new experimental paradigms.

At the same time, however, phenomenology should also be open to the findings of these disciplines. The phenomenological credo 'To the things themselves' calls for us to let our experience guide our theories. We should pay attention to how objects appear to us in experience. Empirical scientists might not pay much attention to deep philosophical questions, but as empirical researchers they do in fact pay quite a lot of attention to concrete phenomena and might consequently be less apt to underestimate the richness, complexity, and variety of the phenomena than the standard armchair philosopher. Empirical science can present phenomenology with concrete findings that it cannot simply ignore, but must be able to accommodate; evidence that might force it to refine or revise its own analyses. The influence can consequently go both ways. In practical terms, what this means is not only that one as a phenomenologist can profit from interdisciplinary collaboration, since one can learn quite a lot about the issues in question by a study of the empirical findings. There is also something deeply satisfying about seeing how a phenomenological analysis of, for example, self-consciousness, shame, or empathy can be of relevance for and inspiration to empirical researchers, be they psychiatrists, developmental psychologists, or anthropologists.

That phenomenology and empirical science can engage (and has engaged) in fruitful collaboration is not to deny their difference. There is no incoherence in claiming that phenomenology should be informed by the best available scientific knowledge, while at the same time insisting that the ultimate transcendental philosophical concerns of phenomenology differ from those of positive science (cf. Zahavi 2010b).

4.-5. What have been the most significant advances in phenomenology? What are the most important open problems and what are the prospects for progress?

During its history, phenomenology has made important contributions to most areas of philosophy, including transcendental philosophy, philosophy of mind, social philosophy, philosophical anthropology, aesthetics, ethics, philosophy of science, epistemology, theory of meaning, and formal ontology. It has provided groundbreaking analyses of such topics as intentionality, perception, embodiment, self-awareness, intersubjectivity and temporality. It has delivered a targeted criticism of reductionism, objectivism and scientism, emphasized the importance of the first-person perspective, and argued at length for a rehabilitation of the life-world. By presenting a detailed account of human existence, where the subject is understood as an embodied and socially and culturally embedded being-in-the-world, phenomenology has also provided important inputs to a whole range of empirical disciplines, including psychiatry, nursing, sociology, architecture, ethnology, and developmental psychology.

Obviously, phenomenology did not end with the death of Merleau-Ponty, Heidegger and Sartre. Much has happened since their seminal works, particularly in French phenomenology. Thinkers like Paul Ricoeur, Michel Henry, Jacques Derrida, Emmanuel Lévinas and Jean-Luc Marion have all questioned the adequacy of many of the classical phenomenological analyses. In their attempt to radicalise phenomenology, they have disclosed new types and structures of manifestation, and thereby made important contributions to the development of phenomenology.

Currently, however, I think phenomenology finds itself at the crossroads. It continues to remain a source of inspiration for other disciplines, and at least certain of its ideas have also been taken up by analytic philosophy and cognitive science. At the same time, phenomenology remains under attack from a variety of different positions, including hard-nosed naturalism and neurocentrism, and after the death of Henry, Levinas and Derrida it is not clear who their natural successors are. It is not easy to identify new thinkers who in equal measures are innovating phenomenology. What we rather find is a lot of good work being done in two directions: inward (and backward) and outward (and forward) (cf. Zahavi 2012). On the one hand, we find a continuing engagement and conversation with the founding fathers (and mothers). The philosophical resources and insights to be found in Husserl's, Heidegger's and Merleau-Ponty's work are evidently not yet exhausted. On the other hand, an increasing amount of dialogue is taking place between phenomenology and other philosophical tradition and empirical disciplines.

The future prospects of phenomenology will obviously depend upon the talent of those who take it up. It is hard to predict how many self-avowed phenomenologists there will be 100 years from now. But I am quite confident that the basic insights found in phenomenology will continue to appeal to and attract and inspire talented thinkers. In fact, if there is any truth to phenomenology, we must be confident that it will be able to renew itself, and continue to flourish in new forms and perhaps also under new names.

About the Editors

Felipe León, b. 1984, is a postdoc at the Center for Subjectivity Research, University of Copenhagen, where he obtained his PhD degree in Philosophy in 2016. León's main areas of research are classical phenomenology, social cognition, and collective intentionality. He is currently part of the project 'You and We: Second-Person Engagement and Collective Intentionality', hosted by the Center for Subjectivity Research, and funded by the Independent Research Fund Denmark. León's publications include 'Shame and Selfhood' (*Phänomenologische Forschungen*. p. 193-211, Jahrgang 2012), 'Experiential Other-Directness: To What Does It Amount?' (*Tidsskrift for Medier, Erkendelse og Formidling*. 1, 1, p. 21-38, 2013), 'Phenomenology of experiential sharing: The contribution of Schutz and Walther' (with Dan Zahavi, in: Salice, A. & Schmid, H. B. (eds.) *The Phenomenological Approach to Social Reality: History, Concepts, Problems*, p. 219-234, 2016), 'For-me-ness, For-us-ness, and the We-relationship' (*Topoi*, doi: 10.1007/s11245-018-9556-2, 2018), and the book *Dación y reflexión: Una investigación fenomenológica* (National University of Colombia, 2016).

Joona Taipale, b. 1978, is a University Lecturer in Philosophy, an Adjunct Professor in Philosophy and a Kone Foundation Experienced Researcher affiliated to the University of Jyväskylä (Finland). Taipale received his Ph.D. from the University of Helsinki in 2009, with a thesis on Husserlian Phenomenology. Since then, he has been employed at the Center for Subjectivity Research (University of Copenhagen, Denmark). Currently he is directing an interdisciplinary research project affiliated to the University of Jyväskylä, University of Helsinki, and Aalto University. Taipale is the author of *Phenomenology and Embodiment* (Northwestern University Press, 2014), and he has published several articles in philosophy and psychology, on topics ranging from empathy, social cognition, and interpersonal understanding, to psychopathology, intersubjectivity, and selfhood. His most recent publications include 'Beyond Cartesianism. Body-perception and the immediacy of empathy' (*Continental Philosophy Review*, 2015), 'Self-regulation and beyond. Affect regulation and the infant-caregiver dyad' (*Frontiers in Psychology*, 2016), 'The structure of group identification' (*Topoi*, 2017)', and 'Controlling the uncontrollable. Self-regulation and the dynamics of addiction' (*Scandinavian Psychoanalytic Review*, 2017).

www.ingramcontent.com/pod-product-compliance
Lightning Source LLC
Chambersburg PA
CBHW021843220426
43663CB00005B/374